I HATE MY LIFE

WINNING THE WAR AGAINST
COVETOUSNESS & DISCONTENT

JACQUELINE E. MCCULLOUGH

J.E. McCullough, LLC
Proclamation | Publishing
2019

Also By Jacqueline E. McCullough:

Daily Moments With God: In Quietness & Confidence
105 Days of Prayer
Satisfaction of the Soul
The Other Side of This

Dedication

I HAVE BEEN the recipient of rich nurturing and godly counsel. This kind of saturated pouring into my life and spirit came from the heart and soul of my late mother, Evangelist Keturah Elizabeth Phillips and my father, the late Reverend Percival Heron Gravel Phillips. They, and a host of mothers from my former church, the St. John Pentecostal Church, including my godmother, Eva Foggie, and my youth leader, Evangelist Shirley Watson — were instrumental in shaping my life.

Along with many professional mentors in the nursing and business arena, this cloud of witnesses guided my life with their wisdom and knowledge. This book, however, is fully dedicated to the memory of my mom, who lived to be 105 years. She taught me a wonderful lesson in my early years.

We were very poor, living in the inner city of Kingston, Jamaica, West Indies. Yet on Sunday mornings, we were dressed in our Sunday's best for Sunday school and church. Mom knew how to take our humble wardrobe and make us feel very special when we wore our dresses. Every now and then, however, my sister and I would notice another girl who had on a fancier and more expensive looking dress and shoes. On those occasions, we would mention to Mom how small and insignificant we felt in the presence of this person. One day, she poured out the wisdom of life that has carried me through to this day. She said, "If you want her dress, then you must settle for everything that she is or is not, where she is or is not going, and how short or long her lifetime." She went on to emphasize this point by saying:

> *"God has your life planned just for you and for His purpose. Accept it and enjoy it. Celebrate God's goodness to you! Always remember to celebrate others and their blessings."*

This lesson was the beginning of my contentment journey through life.

I hope this book will truly reflect the counsel of my mother from the Word and wisdom of God. I pass it on as a legacy to the next generation, hoping that they will find their rest in the Lord.

Contents

PREFACE

The Enough of God

How great is the goodness of God
He is my all sufficient Source
He gives me what I need
He fills me to be free
There is no other place to go and
Find great peace and joy
But to the Fountain rich and pure
From which I will always draw
- J. MCCULLOUGH

I AM PUSHED and goaded by the Holy Spirit to write this book about **contentment**. I earnestly believe that we are living in a time when the Church is experiencing a great falling away because many are not happy with God, His Word, His way and His Church.

I struggled with the title of this book, because of the potential turnoff for readers. I considered the fact that people may be looking for a more upbeat title and not something that would make them uncomfortable. I tried to think of a title that would really reflect the content and purpose of this book that has marinated in my spirit for years. Just when I was about to change it, I started studying the second chapter of Ecclesiastes while preparing for a message. It was there that I found this verse which confirmed the title of this book for me. It is Ecclesiastes 2:17:

> "Therefore *I hated life*; because the work that is wrought under the sun is grievous unto me: for all is vanity and vexation of spirit."

This verse cannot be appreciated unless you read the whole second chapter of Ecclesiastes. First, this is a wisdom book of the Bible, which means it was written by Solomon, the wisest man, to examine the various questions and challenges of life. In it, he grapples with his own experiences and then shares how he reaches a godly conclusion after much disappointment and dissatisfaction.

Second, Solomon was not only the wisest, but one of the richest men of his time. You may view him as a modern-day Bill Gates. He was prosperous, famous, powerful, accomplished and apparently very successful. He stated in the tenth verse of Chapter Two that anything his eyes desired he acquired it. He did not restrain himself from anything and he took great pleasure in his accomplishments. He was so successful that he built one of the Seven Wonders of the World, which is known as Solomon's Temple. However, he concluded that his riches and accomplishments did not bring him lasting joy and satisfaction, but only vanity and vexation of spirit.

What is "vanity"? The Hebrew word is *hebel* (OT:1892 "heh'bel") which means "emptiness, worthlessness, unsatisfactory."[1] His other evaluation of his experiences is

1   Biblesoft's New Exhaustive Strong's Numbers and Concordance with Expanded Greek-Hebrew Dictionary. © 1994, Biblesoft and International Bible Translators, Inc.

that they brought "vexation of spirit." The Hebrew word is OT:7462 *ra` ah* (raw-aw') which is translated "striving or yearning."[2] This suggests reaching after but never satisfied, which can cause one to be vexed or disgruntled. Can you identify with Solomon's sentiment?

The hatred that Solomon had of his life stems from the Hebrew root, *sane*. This type of hate describes an emotional reaction of repulsion and aversion. It is a feeling of strong antagonism and dislike, generally malevolent and prompting to injury (the opposite of love); sometimes born of moral resentment. Skip Moen notes,

> "Hatred entails distance from that which is regarded as undesirable, or utterly unappealing. It is just the opposite of love which brings about the desire for closeness. In this state, a person wishes only to keep distant from the offense or the offender."[3]

Solomon's offender in this case, however, was life. As he contemplated injustice, life, death and issues of equity, the entire consideration made him weary, dispirited, and resigned to life. It filled him with a sense of loathing, resentment, anger and depression. He did not embrace life or celebrate it, but was only repelled and discouraged by it.

When I looked at the fact that this rich, wise and successful man hated his life because material things did not complete him, I decided that I would keep the title of the book. Because if Solomon felt this way, and I have felt this way, then it is quite possible that there are readers who may feel the same way.

---

2   Ibid.
3   https://www.skipmoen.com/2014/03/esau-have-i-hated.

Solomon gave the solution to his discontentment. In this book, I will attempt to bring biblical and godly answers to the vexing issues of a discontented soul.

The Fruit of Faith

The ability to walk with God, obey God and submit to His will is borne out of our belief in Him as Savior, Provider, Healer and Sustainer of our lives. Scripture states in Hebrews 11:6,

> "But without faith it is impossible to please him: for he that cometh to God must believe that he is, and that he is a rewarder of them that diligently seek him."

This passage directs us to the crux of our religious association—Faith.

Faith is confidence, assurance and fidelity in the Person and work of Jesus Christ. To believe in Him and be committed to Him, we must learn about Him. The Bible is where we can obtain what we need to know about Jesus so that we can practice our faith daily. The Bible says in John 20:31, "But these are written, that ye might believe that Jesus is the Christ, the Son of God; and that believing ye might have life through his name."

Found in *Christianity Today* is an October 16, 2018 article written by Jeremy Weber which examines the state of American theology -- "Christian, What Do You Believe? Probably a Heresy About Jesus." Based on a survey released by Ligonier Ministries and LifeWay Research, this third study of its kind examines 34 beliefs, stating,

> "American evangelicals are 'deeply confused' about some core doctrines of the Christian faith—and the

fourth-century heretic Arius would be pleased, according to a new survey."

The research was determined by interviews of about 3,000 Americans to discover what they really believe about God and the Bible. The survey noted that many believed that Jesus died on the Cross and was resurrected. But the core beliefs that the Bible teaches about sin, the Church and the Holy Spirit were rejected by many.

Sadly enough, as the article above alluded, many professed believers have conflicting views about the basic teachings of the Christian Faith.

What one believes will determine what one does. This lack of knowledge or rejection of biblical teachings will produce a lack of faith because Romans 10:17 says, "So then faith cometh by hearing, and hearing by the word of God." The hearing, reading, teaching and preaching of the Word is designed to give the Holy Spirit the tools He needs to convict, convince and show us how we can live honestly and continually with our faith in Jesus Christ. The Word of God comes to cleanse us, guide us and bring us into a closer relationship with the Lord.

The psalmist declares in Psalm 119:105, "Thy word is a lamp unto my feet, and a light unto my path." Just imagine trying to find something in a totally dark room. It is an exercise in futility. It brings frustration and produces defeat. We live in a world filled with darkness. Therefore, we need the light and guidance of the Word of God to show us the way.

The Word of God is also a deterrent to sin and destruction. We were born with the desire to ignore and disobey God's command, but when we accept Christ as Savior and Lord, we can experience the desire to obey and please Him.

The only way to do this is to pile up the Word in our hearts daily. Psalm 119:11 declares: "Thy word have I hid in mine heart, that I might not sin against thee." The word "hid" means "to treasure up or to regard it as the most valuable thing in life." This approach will guard my heart and mind from sinning or straying away from God's command.

You may say, "How do I practice this walk with the Lord?" Well, continue reading this book and you will discover what it takes to have a life of rest and satisfaction in the Lord Jesus Christ.

The only way to persevere in the Christian faith, walk and lifestyle is to yield to the pulling and drawing of the Holy Spirit, Who uses the Word to bind our hearts to the Lord. This is His job; this is what He came to do inside of every believer. Without this ongoing activity of the Word and the Spirit moving in us and through us, we will stray away from the God we say we love.

I have had many days of trials, difficulties and disappointments, but the Lord guided me through them with His Word and His Spirit. He has given me comfort, rest and assurance during the most heart-wrenching moments.

The second week of April 2016, I awoke to what I thought would be an ordinary day. I was summoned by my mother's home attendant to come to Mom's bedside. My mother, who had reached the age of 105, was very dear to my heart. But in that moment, she was unresponsive. I ran hastily to her bed and saw that her eyes were fixed; she was cold and would not speak. I screamed, "Mom, please come back, please respond!" She revived and made eye contact, turned her head and came back to us.

A week later, when no one was in the room for a short space of time, Mom slipped away into eternity. When I entered the room and saw her peacefully resting, knowing that I would never see her or hear her on this side of heaven, I broke. Yes, my heart melted and I wanted to resuscitate her and bring her back to me. It was the Word of God, the presence of Lord and the strength of His arms that carried me through that defining moment. If I did not have faith in God and in the promise of eternal life, I would not have made it through with a peace that could not be explained.

Reader, who you believe in and what you believe will determine your life and response to life's circumstances. This book hopes to press into your heart and mind the necessity to believe, to know, to live and to practice your religion so that you will benefit from your relationship with the Lord. Please remember Jesus' admonition to His followers in Luke 12:15 as you thumb through these pages:

> *"And he said unto them, Take heed, and beware of covetousness: for a man's life consisteth not in the abundance of the things which he possesseth."*

The real value in life is following the Lifegiver's teachings and guidance. Who is this Lifegiver? The Lord Jesus Christ, the Author and Giver of eternal life.

XVIII   I HATE MY LIFE

CHAPTER ONE

The Peril of Unbelief

"THEN THEY DESPISED THE PLEASANT LAND; THEY DID NOT BELIEVE IN HIS WORD: BUT GRUMBLED IN THEIR TENTS; THEY DID NOT LISTEN TO THE VOICE OF THE LORD. THEREFORE HE SWORE TO THEM THAT HE WOULD CAST THEM DOWN IN THE WILDERNESS...."
PSALM 106:24-26

THERE IS a reason why we do what we do. Often, we question within ourselves, "I don't know why I did, said, or behaved like that." The answer may not be apparent to us, but there is an underlying cause for every response.

We will examine the aspects of discontentment in another chapter, but now we have to look at the source of why we cannot be happy or at peace with who we are and Whose we are. Let us identify the reason for the restlessness in our spirits that causes us to disbelieve and doubt God's plan for our lives. If something in us is going to be dealt with, we must go back to the source.

Let's say Jane is having back pains, and she has tried everything to relieve herself of the pain, but it continues. She has tried over-the-counter drugs and lots of home remedies, but to no avail. She finally goes to the doctor, who conducts several tests to determine the source of the pain. As a result of the tests, she learns about a pulled muscle which requires an entirely different treatment from what she thought would be diagnosed. She is now on her way to recovery and the therapy prescribed is relieving her of her discomfort.

To determine why Israel was discontented with God's plan, we have to identify the source — which was unbelief.

Let us examine our opening psalm by exploring the backdrop to its report. It is rehearsing the journey of the children of Israel as they moved out of Egypt under the leadership of Moses. In John C. Maxwell's book, *Think on These Things,* he asks, "Which Tent Do You Live In?" and declares,

> "All men live in one of two tents—content or discontent. In which do you live? The contented man looks beyond his circumstances and sees a better day; the discontented man looks at his circumstances and sees no other way."[4]

The children of Israel's discontentment started with unbelief.

What is Unbelief?

The *International Standard Bible Dictionary* describes unbelief this way:

> "The word (the King James Version) represents two Greek words, *apeitheia*, 'disobedience'...and *apistia*, 'distrust,' the antithesis to 'faith'". [5]

---

4   Maxwell, John C. *Think on These Things: Meditations for Leaders.* 1979, 1999. Beacon Hill Press.

5   "Unbelief." Bromiley, Geoffrey W., Ed. *International Standard Bible Dictionary.* 1988. Grand Rapids, MI: Eerdmans.

The word "unbelief" connotes disobedience and an obstinate rebellious response to God and His command. We often play down the sinfulness of unbelief in light of other more "serious" offenses, such as lying, stealing, murder and adultery. But God looks at unbelief in the same light as any other sinful thought, word or deed which proceeds from our heart. You may say, "I just cannot believe that God would punish me or deal with my unbelief in the same way He would or should deal with a serial killer." Humanly, it seems unfair and unjust, especially if you are not looking at God in the way He is and how He operates from a biblical prospective.

I am not talking about moments of unbelief when we face seemingly impossible situations. We all, as believers, find ourselves grappling with thoughts of "...*Where is God in this? ...How am I going to get out of this? ...Does God really care about me? ...How long do I have to go through this?*" These are the usual emotions that motivate us to question God and doubt His love and power. The true believer, however, comes out of those thoughts one way or another and does not continue to doubt the character, Word and purpose of God. The praying believer will bounce back through prayer, worship and counsel. The unbelief that we are looking at in this text is a continued state of Israel's rebellion and a refusal to change their minds concerning the plan and will of God for their lives.

The children of Israel were given specific instructions, yet they chose not to accept them or execute them. This is a perfect example of how our human heart can hear God, prove God and still reject God by refusing to obey Him. What was God's instruction to the Nation of Israel after He brought them out of the land of Egypt miraculously through

the Red Sea? The scripture in this passage gives us the plan
of God for His nation in Exodus 6:6-8,

> "Wherefore say unto the children of Israel, I am the
> Lord, and I will bring you out from under the burdens
> of the Egyptians, and I will rid you out of their bond-
> age, and I will redeem you with a stretched out arm,
> and with great judgments: And I will take you to me
> for a people, and I will be to you a God: and ye shall
> know that I am the Lord your God, which bringeth
> you out from under the burdens of the Egyptians.
> And I will bring you in unto the land, concerning the
> which I did swear to give it to Abraham, to Isaac, and
> to Jacob; and I will give it you for an heritage: I am the
> Lord."

These people were slaves, with a mentality of bondage,
yet He made such a promise to them and to their children.
Why? He had promised to do so to their forefathers Abraham, Isaac, Jacob, Joseph and Judah. God had a covenant relationship with their ancestors and made promises to them
which would travel from generation to generation. He fulfilled this promise, brought them out of bondage and gave
them further instructions.

The instructions were, according to Deuteronomy 1:6-8,
to go and possess, inherit and occupy the land which the
Lord had prepared for them and their children. The promise was sure because it was given to them from God Who
cannot lie (Numbers 23:19). He does not have the human
flaws, inconsistencies and weaknesses; therefore, He is
able to be consistent and trustworthy. The promise of a
new land, new status and new provision was sure. All they

had to do was to believe and follow His instructions.

I recall numerous times when I did not follow Him and ended up paying an awful price for my disobedience. One particular instance comes to mind concerning my desire to invest in real estate. I connected with a banker from my local bank and mentioned my interest. He informed me of a piece of property that he would assist me in securing without a lot of difficulty. On my way out of the bank, a fellow bank officer pulled me aside and warned me not to trust him, because he was a reckless investor, which could cause me financial embarrassment. When she said it, I heard something strong in my spirit and became disconcerted in my thoughts, but strongly brushed it off, even though it lingered for days.

In spite of the lingering, I pursued the acquisition of this property. To my chagrin, I suffered a great financial loss and embarrassment, which took years for me to recover. I cannot say that the Lord, through the gentle voice of the bank officer, did not warn or instruct me. I chose to follow my own desire, ambition and drive to have real estate, rather than to wait on the Lord. It does not mean that the Lord did not want me to own property, but He wanted me to do it in His way and in His time. I am sure that you can remember times that you ignored the prodding of the Holy Spirit and moved in a different direction, which led to grave consequences. Thanks be to God, I was able to move on with much clarity and understanding, which served as a guidepost for future decisions.

The Consequence of Unbelief

I am blessed at this time in my life to have quite a few members of the next generation in my life. They are in my home, my bed, my closet, my refrigerator, and just in my life. As a result, I have the opportunity to walk with them and to pour into them in a very personal and intentional manner.

One of the crucial lessons that they are learning is that with every action there is reaction, which we call "consequence." They learned early on that whatever they did, positive or negative, there would be an effect afterwards. There is a certain spot in a certain room in the house which we call "The Time Out Spot." Many of them have spent their special moments rethinking their decisions and actions in that special location. They may have had to spend time in that space for the same reason until they finally seemed to understand that the negative behavior was unacceptable. The converse is also true that we have celebrated their obedience by reaffirming their godly decisions and encouraging them to continue.

Well, believers are no different from these little people. We, too, have to face the consequences of our actions while we are on earth. We are admonished in Hebrews 3:15-19,

> "While it is said, Today if ye will hear his voice, harden not your hearts, as in the provocation. For some, when they had heard, did provoke: howbeit not all that came out of Egypt by Moses. But with whom was he grieved forty years? was it not with them that had sinned, whose carcases fell in the wilderness? And to whom sware he that they should not enter into his rest, but to them that believed not? So we see that they could not enter in because of unbelief."

This passage of scripture gives us the result of rejecting, ignoring and disobeying God's Word and command.

It does not mean that our unbelief can stop God from doing what He intends to do, because He is in charge. However, we will not benefit from the promises that are awarded to those who trust Him. As a result of their unbelief, the older generation did not possess the Promised Land, but their children age 40 years and younger entered and gained the land. It shows that God did not fail to deliver His promise, but those who did not believe forfeited their inheritance.

In Jesus' time, the unbelief of the people of Nazareth caused them to lose out on experiencing Jesus' miraculous power. The Bible says in Matthew 13:57-58,

> "And they were offended in him. But Jesus said unto them, A prophet is not without honour, save in his own country, and in his own house. And he did not many mighty works there because of their unbelief."

I understand that you could be in a difficult place and perhaps your expectation of God's help is not being met. But please, do not give in or give up, because God will not forget or forsake you, even if it feels that way. We must remember that God is entirely trustworthy and that He cannot lie. He is unchangeable, immutable and steadfast. It is not that He *will not* lie, but it is that He *cannot* lie (Hebrews 16:18). Let us not downplay our disbelief of God, but let us guard our hearts to be careful to trust His Word and His character. To banish unbelief, let us affirm and reaffirm His perfect wisdom and His goodness. Grab your Bible, along with your journal or wherever you write your personal notes, and listen for God's encouragement and assurance. As you draw nigh to Him, He will strengthen your faith in Him.

Walking in Obedience and Belief

How do I live a life of obedience? The first thing we must do is to agree that God is sovereign and that He knows how to govern our lives. It is key that we fully embrace the concept that we are not called to govern ourselves. The realization that we are obligated to obey Him because He is the Creator and we are His creatures, is stated in Psalm 95:6,

> "O come, let us worship and bow down: let us kneel before the Lord our maker."

We have His Word and commandments which are clearly revealed; therefore, we have no excuse to disbelieve or disobey Him. Consider how the Father has equipped us to believe:

1. He grants unto us His exceeding great and precious promises (2 Peter 1:4).
2. This ability was given to us because Christ died for us (Galatians 2:20).
3. The Holy Spirit dwells in us to help us (1 Corinthians 6:19).

As a result, this obedience provides subsequent blessings.

The Blessings of Obedience and Belief:

1. We experience a testimony of transformation (2 Corinthians 5:17).
2. Peace of mind and heart are produced in our lives (Psalm 25:12-13).
3. We receive the favor of God (Isaiah 1:19).

4. We partake of the promise of life eternal (Romans 6:22-23).

The evidence that we are content and are in agreement with God is displayed in how ready we are to submit our will, opinions and preferences to His Word and His way.

Let us draw near with a true heart in full assurance of faith, having our hearts sprinkled from an evil conscience, and our bodies washed with pure water. Let us hold fast the profession of our faith without wavering;
(for he is faithful that promised).
HEBREWS 10:22-23

CHAPTER TWO

The Futility of Discontent

"THEN THEY DESPISED THE PLEASANT LAND; THEY DID NOT
BELIEVE IN HIS WORD, BUT GRUMBLED IN THEIR TENTS; THEY
DID NOT LISTEN TO THE VOICE OF THE LORD. THEREFORE HE
SWORE TO THEM THAT HE WOULD CAST THEM DOWN IN THE
WILDERNESS...."
PSALM 106:24-26

I N CHAPTER One, we looked at the root of why we often
feel so frustrated with our lives and with the way God is
operating in our lives. Our opening psalm is a great example of the feeling, language, reason and consequences of
discontent. We will look at these aspects closely and see if
we can walk away with a peace with God in our souls.

What is Discontent?

As discussed previously, John C. Maxwell continues the
question from his book, *Think on These Things*,

> "All men live in one of two tents—content or discontent. In which do you live? ...The contented man is anchored to clear goals and is hardly ever swayed; the discontented man has no goals that anchor him and is many times dismayed." [6]

6 Maxwell, J. C. *Think on These Things: Meditations for Leaders.* 1979, 1999.
Kansas City: Beacon Hill Press.

This feeling of dismay and hopelessness has to be examined if we are going to walk away from the nagging, tormenting notion of helplessness that discontent, also termed "discontentment," brings. The definition of this noun is "unhappiness caused by the failure of one's hopes, desires, or expectations: disappointment, discontent, disgruntlement, dissatisfaction, letdown or regret," according to *The American Heritage® Roget's Thesaurus.*

This definition is the picture of someone who is not content with life. Because of failed desires and hopes, they are on the precipice of depression and despair. Therefore, we must look closely at what contentment looks like. In the Hebrew, the concept of being "satisfied" can suffice for our understanding and observation. *Vines' Dictionary* defines "satisfaction" from the Hebrew word *saba*`. It describes the person's soul as being "filled, or fully sated." God declares in Psalm 107:9, "For he satisfieth the longing soul, and filleth the hungry soul with goodness."

The notion of having one's soul satisfied is clearly seen when Jesus had His discourse with the woman at the well in Samaria in John 4:13-14. This meeting brought the woman face-to-face with her need for a different kind of inner satisfaction. The metaphor used was "water." This water was identified by Jesus as "living water," which meant that she would experience another kind of life. This spiritual life would come from having a relationship with Jesus and would cause her to never look to anyone else to fill her soul, but Jesus.

Again, the water referenced meant the life of Christ versus the empty offerings of the world, which gives a temporary feeling of fullness, but soon empties out. Jesus is the only One Who can give the soul, the heart and the mind sustaining peace, joy and satisfaction.

Discontent brings anxiety, frustration and continuing vanity. There is no lasting peace or rest to the soul, which heightens the need to search for more here and there.

For many people, getting older can be a great source of discontentment. They may feel that life has passed them by and that there were certain goals that they should have accomplished by a certain time in their life. This discontent can bring on depression, discouragement and despair. However, age should not be the deciding factor for our life and future. There are many people who discover their true talent and purpose much later in life.

When I was a nursing student, most of my classmates were in their twenties along with me. But there was an older woman in her forties that I'll call "Miss P," who was attending classes with us. While we, in our youthful manner, studied carelessly and sought free time frequently, Miss P was often found in the library or talking after class with the professors. We were busy seeking ways to avoid extra work and shortcut our responsibilities. Well, this woman was more focused, intentional and successful. Many younger students failed, dropped out, or had emotional breakdowns. But Miss P graduated with a 4.0 average and was known as one of the best student nurses in her clinical experience. Age did not stop her, nor did she allow her past experiences to cause discontentment and discouragement.

Reader, I pray that you would stop right now and examine yourself in this area of dissatisfaction and see where it is lurking in your heart so that the Lord can give you answers and direction. The solution or remedy for the feeling of discontentment or dissatisfaction can be dealt with by applying biblical truths:

1. Trust God and not self (Proverbs 3:5-6).
2. Think differently (Philippians 4:8).
3. Worship at all times (Psalm 42:5).
4. Be thankful (1 Thessalonians 5:18).
5. Agree with God (Romans 8:28).

These are just a few daily practices that will confront and neutralize the feelings of fear, disappointment, and despair.

Feelings of Discontent

Everything we prayed about, I was feeling for the past couple of days. Discouraged, and discontentment. Not agreeing with His sovereignty. I felt like I suffered long enough. ...Yeah, this feeling is not fun at all. It makes me heavy and literally all I want to do is give up ... but deep down I know I have to press. I just don't understand why I have to go through ALL OF THIS PRESSING AND everyone around me is getting what they want. My insecurities are clouding my vision. I honestly don't believe deep down that there's something for me to do in the Kingdom. I really do hate my life. - C.A.B.

One of the ways we express our discontent is through our emotions and feelings. We see this concept clearly in the way the children of Israel responded to the challenge of going to possess the land of Canaan. Psalm 106:24 says, "Yea, they despised the pleasant land, they believed not his word." The word "despised" in this verse describes an intense negative emotion of repulsion released by God's covenant people. *Strong's Exhaustive Concordance* translates this word as OT:3988 *ma'ac*, which means "to reject, refuse, despise."

Their inward repulsion and refusal of the promise may have been the result of their time spent in Egypt, which was over 400 years. The bottom line is that they rebelled against the will, purpose and plan of God. This kind of feeling is strong, powerful and consuming. It influenced and motivated the Hebrews to hate, reject and refuse the Word and promise of the Lord.

This desire to negate God's sovereignty and providence is an inherited tendency borne out of the sin nature passed through the bloodline of Adam and Eve. From the expulsion from the Garden of Eden to the present, humans have continually despised and rejected God's sovereign rule in the world and in their lives. The Bible states in Romans 3:23, "For all have sinned, and come short of the glory of God." This innate propensity to disobey God and become hostile towards Him is a natural response. It is not a surprise that the children of Israel would find it so easy to reject the glorious promise of possession of the land of Canaan.

This Promised Land was glorious because God said it was. It was also described as a "pleasant" land, which means "good, fertile and delightful." God describes the land in Exodus 3:8,

> "And I am come down to deliver them out of the hand of the Egyptians, and to bring them up out of that land unto a good land and a large, unto a land flowing with milk and honey; unto the place of the Canaanites, and the Hittites, and the Amorites, and the Perizzites, and the Hivites, and the Jebusites."

Yet, in spite of the goodness of the land, the fertility of the soil, and the harvest of the fruits, they could not accept and enjoy God's blessings. Everything in them rejected it.

Discontentment is usually fueled by strong emotions. For a number of years, I have attended a Good Friday Service sponsored by Church Women United in Brooklyn, New York. Seven leading female ministers speak on the Seven Last Words of Jesus from the Cross. One of the speakers stated that "feelings lie, but the Word tells the truth." I never forgot that statement. I know that my feelings lie to me on a regular basis. My heart has responded to what I saw and not what I knew. It is the state and matter of the heart that creates the feelings. Proverbs 23:7 states, "For as he thinketh in his heart, so is he...." The word "thinketh" in the Hebrew is *sha`ar* (shaw-ar') which means "to estimate, calculate, to divide; to decipher; to come to conclusion."[7] Therefore, the manner in which we comb through a thought, desire, wish or feeling in our minds will determine how we will perform.

Does God ignore our feelings? Should we acknowledge or respond to our emotions? There is a popular saying that states, "Go with what you feel!" Another saying I have heard for many years is that one should "follow their heart." What does the Bible say about feelings and the heart's desire? The word "heart" in the Hebrew as found in *Strong's Dictionary* is *leb* OT:3820[8] which also signifies the mind. It also can be used of the inner man, contrasted to the outer man, as in Deuteronomy 30:14: "But the word is very nigh unto thee, in thy mouth, and in thy heart, that thou mayest do it." You can also see God's description of the true nature of man as being the state of his heart in 1 Samuel 16:7:

7   Strong, James. Strong's Exhaustive Concordance of the Bible. Iowa Falls, Iowa: World Bible Publishers, 1986.
8 Ibid.

> "But the Lord said unto Samuel, Look not on his countenance, or on the height of his stature; because I have refused him: for the Lord seeth not as man seeth; for man looketh on the outward appearance, but the Lord looketh on the heart."

The heart is also viewed as the seat of emotions as expressed in Deuteronomy 6:5-6:

> "And thou shalt love the Lord thy God with all thine heart, and with all thy soul, and with all thy might And these words, which I command thee this day, shall be in thine heart."

The heart is the housing place of our thoughts, feelings desires, hopes, dreams, pain and disappointment, to name a few. The Greek word for "heart" is *kardia*[9] (kar-dee'-ah) which refers to "the thoughts or feelings or mind." It is impossible to separate one's feelings or thoughts from one's mind. Therefore, the feeling of discontentment is birthed in the heart and mind of the individual. This feeling must be identified and explored if we are going to deal with the uneasiness and unhappiness that come with not being satisfied. Since the feeling is propelled by the inner man, we should look at what God says in His Word about the seat of our emotions. God says in Jeremiah 17:9-10:

> "The heart is deceitful above all things, and desperately wicked: who can know it? I the Lord search the heart, I try the reins, even to give every man according to his ways, and according to the fruit of his doings."

---

9   Ibid.

Let us look at some key words in these verses! First, the word "deceitful" is a description of the human heart, and means "crooked, fraudulent, twisted." Secondly, the heart is described as "desperately wicked," which means "incurably sick and melancholic." Third, the phrase, "who can know it?" means that the heart is corrupt; some commentators say, "it hides itself from itself." This, my dear readers, is God's diagnosis of man's sinful heart, inherited from Father Adam and Mother Eve. Without the transformation power of the Holy Spirit, this heart of ours cannot be trusted to do good and to embrace truth. This heart then seeks to attach itself to accomplishments, people and things to ease and soothe the misery that such a heart produces. It is no surprise that discontent finds a comfortable place in the compartment of the inside of our being.

This feeling of dissatisfaction is based on what one thinks and believes. Just as Eve fed her mind with what the enemy said to her and rejected or distorted what God said was good for her, the Israelites did not believe that possessing the land that God gave them was for their good. This unbelief persisted even in the face the miracles God had worked in their midst. Robert S. McGee in his book, *The Search for Significance,* addresses Eve's attitude and actions on Page 23:

> "Being deceived, Eve traded God's truth for the serpent's lie. She ate the forbidden fruit. Then Adam followed her in sinful rebellion against God, and he, too, ate the forbidden fruit. One of the tragic implications of this event is that man lost his secure status with God and began to struggle with feelings of arrogance, inadequacy, and despair, valuing the opinions of oth-

ers more than the truth of God. This robbed man of his true self-worth and put him on a continual, but fruitless, search for significance through his success and the approval of others."[10]

The author reminds us of the deep-seated innate desire to follow our feelings, ambitions and drives more than submitting to the all-knowing and ever-loving God.

I have had many, many moments of deep discouragement and hopelessness; but my help came from the Word of God and my deliverance came from my worship. Worship for me is therapeutic. Some people need Happy Hour; others need a yoga class. Many go on a cruise, but I worship. One of the psalms that describe my worship is Psalm 42:5, 11, which gives us an idea of how David struggled with his inner conflicts and out-of-control emotions:

> Why art thou cast down, O my soul? and why art thou disquieted in me? hope thou in God: for I shall yet praise him for the help of his countenance... Why art thou cast down, O my soul? and why art thou disquieted within me? hope thou in God: for I shall yet praise him, who is the health of my countenance, and my God.

Let us glean from these verses how David settled it.

1. Ask your soul the reason for the discontentment, casting down and depression.
2. Inquire within your soul about the reason for the disquietedness, inner rage and tumult within.
3. Tell your soul to hope in the Lord, and to patiently wait on the Lord.

---

10   McGee, Robert S. *The Search for Significance.* Nashville: Thomas Nelson. 2003.

4. Lift up your hands and praise Him, confess Him, reverence Him, and worship Him.
5. As a result, there will be help, healing, deliverance, victory, and prosperity for your face and in your life.

Let this psalm be your way out of momentary or long-standing feelings of despair, because God is able to fill your heart with His desire.

The Language of Discontent

The prolific preacher Charles Spurgeon wrote a meditation from the Apostle Paul's words of Philippians 4:11, "I have learned, in whatever state I am, therewith to be content." Spurgeon states:

> *"...These words show us that contentment is not a natural propensity of man. Its weeds grow apace. Covetousness, discontent, and murmuring are as natural to man as thorns are to the soil. We need not sow thistles and brambles; they come up naturally enough, because they are indigenous to earth: and so, we need not teach men to complain..."*[11]

I am in agreement with Spurgeon that it is quite natural for us to murmur and complain. Discontent has a language and it is called murmuring. Complaining is another offense that most Christians think is minor and inconsequential. People make light of the notion that continual murmuring and complaining against the will, purpose and character of God vexes Him. They see it as a very minor issue and don't think it should be judged or challenged. In their view, it is

11   Spurgeon, C.H. *Morning and Evening.* Peabody, MA: Hendrickson Publishers, 1994.

not as weighty as denouncing God, forsaking God or even sinning against God. Well, let us look at how God viewed the children of Israel's murmuring and see if we can find ourselves in the midst.

Psalm 106:25 states, "But murmured in their tents...." What did they say specifically in their complaint against the Lord? Numbers 14:2, 27 notes,

> "And all the children of Israel murmured against Moses and against Aaron: and the whole congregation said unto them, Would God that we had died in the land of Egypt! or would God we had died in this wilderness!
>
> "How long shall I bear with this evil congregation, which murmur against me? I have heard the murmurings of the children of Israel, which they murmur against me."

These passages prove that murmuring was a definite part of the children of Israel's verbal response to their circumstances.

The word "murmur," according to *Strong's Exhaustive Concordance* is #OT:H7279 *ragan* (raw-gan'); a primitive root; means "to grumble, i.e. rebel." Theologian Albert Barnes declares of the Israelites, "They complained of Moses; they complained of their food; they complained of the hardships of their journey; they complained of God. They did this when "in their tents;" when they had a comfortable home; when safe; when provided for; when under the direct divine protection and care."[12] The commentary cited Israel's lifestyle of complaining and murmuring to express

12   Barnes' Notes, Electronic Database. © 1997 by Biblesoft.

their feelings of dissatisfaction. Although they complained specifically about their conditions, they were ultimately dissatisfied with God.

Ultimately, murmuring declares that *God is not delivering what I want.* There are times when I go out to dinner with friends. A few of these friends can be very difficult to please. I am not suggesting that the customer should not get what he/she desires, but some of the causes for complaints are uncalled for and unjustified. When that happens, I usually hang my head in shame, because the murmuring and complaining had nothing to do with the level of service. It had everything to do with what the person was feeling or going through at that time. You see, the language betrayed the soul, a soul in distress and turmoil.

The Curse of Complaining

What does murmuring and complaining suggest in one's relationship with the Lord?

In the Hebrew, the word "murmuring" is *lun* which denotes the "clearly stated mutterings of disgruntled persons." An example of this is when Korah and his company rebelled against Moses and Aaron, competing for the civil and spiritual leadership to the people of Israel (Numbers 16:8-11). This account showed how the princes of Israel verbally attacked Moses with their complaint and rejection of his leadership. In their challenge, it was not just a verbal attack against Moses and Aaron, but it was an attack against God's decision to choose Moses and Aaron as the leaders of the community.

The *International Standard Bible Encyclopedia* declares that in the three places you find the word "murmur" (Deut. 1:27; Ps. 106:25; Isa. 29:24), it translates a Hebrew word (*raghan*) which suggests the malicious whispering of slander.

Murmuring, then, is more than just negative talk or depressed conversations; it is evil, malicious talk that is designed to attack or destroy something stated or established. For the believer, it is deadly to speak against what God has revealed. We all experience doubt, fear, anxiety and discouragement, but we must watch our constant complaining and evil reporting with our mouths and in our hearts.

It is not just an expression of words, but it is the release of an evil tongue. This tongue loves to speak lies, enjoys boasting and devises deceits.

> "The tongue is an indicator of a person's spirit: it reveals what is in the heart (Matthew 12:33-37; 15:18; Luke 6:43-45). In the classic New Testament passage on the tongue, James warns specifically against the evil of an uncontrolled and uncharitable tongue (James 3:1-12)."[13]

Spurgeon's exhortation mentioned earlier challenges us to be aware of the language of discontentment and dissatisfaction. We are often clueless to the conscious and unconscious ways in which we express our disagreement with God's divine plan and intervention in our lives. I am reminded of how many times the Lord spoke to me from Psalm 19:14 which states:

> "*Let the words of my mouth, and the meditation of my heart, be acceptable in thy sight, O Lord, my strength, and my redeemer.*"

---

13   Nelson's Illustrated Bible Dictionary, © 1986, Thomas Nelson Publishers.

This is a prayer that the psalmist uttered of his desire, wish or hope.   The sayings and expressions from our mouths, which give voice to the issues of our hearts, should be released with much prayer and consideration.

The Language of the Heart

The next portion of Psalm 19:14 is just as important to the prayer, which is the meditation of our hearts. The word "meditate" in the Hebrew connotes "muttering, speaking to oneself in low tones, or speaking softly while musing or thinking on something specific."[14] It reminds of me of what Hannah was doing when she went to her place of prayer and muttered out of the depths of her heart in 1 Samuel 1:12-13. In Hannah's prayer, she was making a heartfelt request to the Lord. The psalmist, however, was praying that his heartfelt desire would please the Lord.

Meditation suggests that there is something very strongly lodged in our minds that holds our preoccupation. These thoughts can often be self-centered, troublesome and wearisome, and could cause us to forget God's benefits, love and promises. It takes the Word of God hidden in our hearts or freshly dropped upon our ears to bring our minds back to His will and His way. This requires sacrifice and learning to discipline ourselves by surrendering our choices to the Lord Jesus.

The essence of the prayer in the psalm is the determined intention to bring delight and pleasure to the Lord by what we say and think. This combined effort of right words and right thinking towards God cannot be done without the strength of the Lord. The Lord is our Rock and our Deliverer.

---

14   Strong, James. Strong's Exhaustive Concordance of the Bible. Iowa Falls, Iowa: World Bible Publishers, 1986.

We can't do what seemingly is difficult and uncomfortable on our own. This kind of walk and talk requires a close and intimate relationship with the Lord through prayer, praise and perseverance. Let us grab our mouths and guard our hearts and minds from wandering away from the secured place that God has for us in Him and His Word.

Causes for Consideration

What should we consider? We should be aware of how complaining words will affect our relationship with the Lord. Useless chatter, disagreeable words, continual complaining and angry venting are just a few of the ways our speech can offend the ears of our Father, damage our faith in our Savior and injure the peace of our mind.

There were times when I spoke carelessly and unthinkingly to the Lord, even in prayer. When I have been stressed and pressed, I would say, "I give You my life, my time and my resources and You neglect to take care of me." This is misguided, tantrum, meltdown talk. There isn't an ounce of truth in those words. He was always there; He was always caring, and He always kept His Word. Of course, the repentance came after I had my blow-up, which caused me much embarrassment and conviction. Scripture says in Numbers 23:19:

> "God is not a man, that he should lie; neither the son of man, that he should repent: hath he said, and shall he not do it? or hath he spoken, and shall he not make it good?"

This is just one of the texts in the Bible that states that God cannot lie and will always keep His Word towards His subjects. It is so easy to forget how powerful, holy, good and righteous God is when we are going through. It is the trick of the enemy to cause us to speak foolishly, arrogantly and in error against the God of our lives.

Please think about how many times we have spoken out of turn to our friends, family, children, co-workers, and even the cashier and many others, because of the state of our hearts and minds. There has to be a consciousness of the ill doings of our tongue, so that we can ask the Holy Spirit to convict us not to go too far out against our Lord with our negative speeches. Here are two verses of a beloved hymn, "Take My Life and Let It Be," written by Frances Havergal:

Verse 1:
Take my life and let it be
Consecrated Lord to Thee,
Take my moments and my days,
Let them flow in endless praise.

Verse 3:
Take my voice and let me sing,
Always, only for my King,
Take my lips and let them be,
Swift and beautiful for Thee.

May this hymn be a part of your daily prayer and devotion, guarding your tongue and quieting your spirit!

Disobedience and Discontentment
I never wanted to be a preacher. My parents were preachers and pastors, but while growing up, it never occurred to me that I should automatically become a preacher and pas-

tor. Well of course, God had that in mind for me and I did become a preacher. I slowly got over that and settled into being an itinerant preacher for many years and traveled extensively doing just that.

The Lord was not finished with me, because He eventually wanted to add the role of pastor to the assignment. I know many people do not believe in female pastors and I do not intend to defend or argue the point. What I am sharing is my human struggle with the responsibility of nurturing and shepherding God's flock. I saw so much irresponsible leadership in this area that I ran from it. Many godly people encouraged and challenged me, and I became adamant and sometimes arrogantly rude when they mentioned the idea of pastoring.

I continued for many years avoiding and ignoring the call on my life to feed, guide and protect God's sheep. The years that I ran caused me much discomfort. I was so miserable in my spirit. I continued preaching, but at the end of the day, I was thoroughly uncomfortable. However, I loved the Lord, so I knew that it was only a matter of time. I know lots of people run to pastor, but to me the pastoral assignment is an awesome task that requires strong commitment and dedication. Well, my days of disobedience came to an end. On one of my mission trips to Jamaica, while speaking at a Bible school in the hills, I burst out passionately that I would submit to the assignment of Pastor. That was 17 years ago. I assure you that while I was disobedient, I was discontented.

Let's be honest as believers! Disobedience and discontent fit each other like a hand in glove. When we are not in agreement with God, it affects our peace of mind and satisfaction of the soul.

Previously we looked at all the other portions of Scripture which considered unbelief, discontentment, feelings of discontent and the language of discontent. Let us now consider the portion of Scripture which talks about hearing and obeying the voice of the Lord. It is vital that we see disobedience as a companion to the dissatisfaction of our soul. When we do, we will be able to eradicate it from our lives.

A Heart to Hearken

The Word says in Psalm 106:25, *"...and hearkened not unto the voice of the Lord."* The Israelites did not obey God by going and possessing the Promised Land. What does this really mean?

The word "hearken" is not a common word in our present-day vernacular and lingo. As we closely examine the meaning of this word in the text, let's see if we can get the gist of how it applied to the ancient people and how it applies to us today.

The *Theological Workbook of the Old Testament* defines the word "hearken" by stating:

> OT:8085 - *sama* has the basic meaning "to hear." This is extended in various ways, generally involving an effective hearing or listening: 1) "listen to"; "pay attention"; 2) "obey" (with words such as "commandment" etc.); 3) "answer prayer, hear"; 4) "understand"; and 5) "hear critically"; "examine (in court)."[15]

All these meanings suggest listening and obeying or taking heed. What then is disobedience? *Nelson's Bible Dictio-*

---

15   Harris, R. Laird; Archer, Gleason L.; Waltke, Bruce. *Theological Workbook of the Old Testament,* 2003. Chicago, IL: Moody.

nary declares disobedience to be "an unwillingness to comply with the guidance of authority, especially a neglect of God's will."[16]

This desire in all humans to defy the authority, Word and will of God received its genesis from Adam and Eve. The third chapter of Genesis talks about the rebellion of Adam and Eve against God's prohibition to not eat of the fruit of the tree of the knowledge of good and evil. When they disobeyed God, that spirit of disobedience passed on through the genes of the whole human race. Scripture notes in Romans 5:19,

> "For as by one man's disobedience many were made sinners, so by the obedience of one shall many be made righteous."

The one man here refers to Adam. His disobedience rendered us unable to obey God and His commands. How many times have I defied the instruction of the Lord in my life? There are more times than I would like to count. I am sure, reader, you have the same confession of times of lack of obedience and submission to God's directives. Rebellion or refusal to acquiesce to God's will and purpose is strongly laced throughout the biblical text. This stubbornness didn't stop in Genesis and it travels all the way to Revelation.

How did the children of Israel refuse to hearken to the voice of the Lord in Psalm 106:25? They were told to go up and possess the land, but as I mentioned before, they refused to go and settle into the land. Yet they were encouraged and challenged by Caleb and Joshua to trust God and follow His command in Numbers 14:6-10:

---

16   *Nelson's Illustrated Bible Dictionary*, (c)1986, Thomas Nelson Publishers.

"And Joshua the son of Nun, and Caleb the son of Je-
phunneh, which were of them that searched the land,
rent their clothes: And they spake unto all the company of the children of Israel, saying, The land, which
we passed through to search it, is an exceeding good
land. If the Lord delight in us, then he will bring us
into this land, and give it us; a land which floweth
with milk and honey. Only rebel not ye against the
Lord, neither fear ye the people of the land; for they
are bread for us: their defence is departed from them,
and the Lord is with us: fear them not. But all the congregation bade stone them with stones. And the glory
of the Lord appeared in the tabernacle of the congregation before all the children of Israel."

The resistance to God's plan for their lives was so strong
that they proceeded to physically attack the men of God.
Violence proceeded out of rebellion. They were afraid,
anxious and insecure. This is seen when 10 of the 12 men
representing 10 of the tribes made their report to the community about their visit to the Promised Land in Numbers
13:32-33:

"And they brought up an evil report of the land which
they had searched unto the children of Israel, saying,
The land, through which we have gone to search it, is
a land that eateth up the inhabitants thereof; and all
the people that we saw in it are men of a great stat-
ure. And there we saw the giants, the sons of Anak,
which come of the giants: and we were in our own
sight as grasshoppers, and so we were in their sight."

The evil report had to do with more than just what they said, but what they refused to believe and obey. Who did they disobey? They disobeyed God, Who gave them the promise, the instruction and the opportunity. How serious is disobedience towards God?

The Dangers of Disobedience

Let's look at how God dealt with disobedience in the Bible. One example is seen in the life of King Saul. The prophet Samuel was sent by God to command Saul to destroy the Amalekites with specific instructions in 1 Samuel 15:2:

> "Thus saith the Lord of hosts, I remember that which Amalek did to Israel, how he laid wait for him in the way, when he came up from Egypt. Now go and smite Amalek, and utterly destroy all that they have, and spare them not; but slay both man and woman, infant and suckling, ox and sheep, camel and ass."

Saul gathered about 300,000 fighters and defeated the Amalekites. But he disobeyed the divine command by taking alive Agag, the king, and sparing all the best of the cattle and all that was valuable, destroying only that which was unacceptable in his sight. Samuel had received the instruction from God to confront the king's disobedience. Samuel went to Saul and asked him if he had carried out God's injunction, but Saul tried to justify his disobedience by affirming that he did obey. He explained to Samuel that the people were responsible for bringing back the animals and that the animals were suitable for sacrifice (1 Samuel 15:19-21).

The evidence of Saul's disobedience was discovered because of the bleating of the sheep and the lowing of the

oxen. Samuel described for Saul and for us how rebellion
appears in the sight of God by saying in 1 Samuel 15:23:

> "For rebellion is as the sin of witchcraft, and stub-
> bornness is as iniquity and idolatry. Because thou
> hast rejected the word of the Lord, he hath also re-
> jected thee from being king."

Let us examine this verse! Rebellion, which is bitterness
and hostility towards God, is as the sin of witchcraft, which
is a practice of getting information or guidance from a pa-
gan god or a source outside of the God of the Bible. The
Israelites were commanded to put to death anyone en-
gaging in the practice (Ex. 22:18), and the major prophets
condemned divination (Isa. 44:24-25). Jeremiah also condemned the practice of witchcraft:

> "Therefore hearken not ye to your prophets, nor to
> your diviners, nor to your dreamers, nor to your en-
> chanters, nor to your sorcerers, which speak unto
> you, saying, Ye shall not serve the king of Babylon"
> (Jeremiah 27:9).

These passages reveal that the prophets condemned the
practice of witchcraft, which Samuel compared to the sin
of rebellion. This clearly means that to rebel against God
or to disobey His Word is the same as looking to another
god or following another god for information and guidance.
The other god, however, is you. To suggest that what God
is requiring is not acceptable is to say that your opinion or
another's opinion is more important than what God has
requested. In that sense, it is equal to going to a witch for
counsel or advice.

Samuel also addresses Saul's stubbornness, which means to "press, push and to urge." Stubborn people are usually very pushy, determined and tenacious. When one is stubborn against God's purpose, the prophet equates that to iniquity and idolatry. Iniquity is defined as wickedness and vanity. It is also as the sin of idolatry, which is the worship of anything created, instead of worshiping the Creator.

There is nothing wrong with being tenacious, determined, focused and persistent. The disobedience, as a believer, comes in when we exemplify these passions against the revealed will and purpose of God in our lives. Disobedience opens the door to more than refusal to do God's will. It leads to greater sin, severe wickedness and gross idolatry. This was not just an Old Testament issue. Jesus also demanded obedience from His disciples and followers in John 14:15, 21:

> "If ye love me, keep my commandments. ...He that hath my commandments, and keepeth them, he it is that loveth me: and he that loveth me shall be loved of my Father, and I will love him, and will manifest myself to him."

Indeed, the Lord demands obedience and commitment from His believers. The bottom line is that when we are rejecting God, we are now accepting another god. Why are we prone to worship the creature rather than the Creator? Edward T. Welch, in his book, *Choices*, gives reasons as to why we neglect the true and living God and resort to devoting our affections to other gods:

> "...We are proud. Isaiah 2:6-22 reveals that idolaters are arrogant. Idolaters, even when they are bowing

down, are 'arrogant,' 'proud,' and 'lofty.' Apparently, our idols are actually intended to exalt ourselves and our own desires. Even in our idolatry we want nothing above ourselves. We choose idols in part because we believe they can give us what we want."[17]

Whether we agree or not, Scripture supports the fact that there is a propensity in all of us to prefer ourselves rather than God. This, my dear reader, is what we call **disobedience.**

---

17   Welch, Edward T. *Choices: Why Do I Do These Things?* Greensboro, NC: New Growth Press. Pp. 26-30.

CHAPTER THREE

Covetousness Breeds Discontent
I WANT WHAT I WANT WHEN I WANT IT!

MY HOME is bursting with the sound of infant cries, racing feet, bouncing balls, whining complaints and giggling laughter. Where is all this commotion coming from? It is coming from the mouths, feet and hands of little people. Yes, they are everywhere, doing what they should not be doing and avoiding what they should be engaged in. Many times, the frequent cry has to do with not getting what they want. The interesting thing is that they do get something, but it is never enough. The biggest fight is over snacks. I must confess that I have done them a disservice by turning them on to a certain cracker, which I eat every now and then. They count how many the other one has received and compare it to what they have received, which usually leads to the cry of discontent.

The issue is not that they did not receive, but that they felt that it was not enough. This feeling was especially pronounced if they saw someone else's portion. This attitude is not just the passion of little people; it is the driving force centered in the human heart of young, old, rich or poor. We need to closely examine the underlying cause of the feelings of dissatisfaction that linger deep in our hearts. What is it? The Bible calls it **"covetousness."**

Merriam-Webster defines covetousness as "greedy, acquisitive, grasping, avaricious, having or showing a strong desire for especially material possessions. Covetousness implies inordinate desire, often for another's possessions."[18] *Nelson's Bible Dictionary* defines it as:

> "An intense desire to possess something (or someone) that belongs to another person. The Ten Commandments prohibit this attitude (Ex. 20:17; Deut. 5:21). Covetousness springs from a greedy self-centeredness and an arrogant disregard of God's law. The Bible repeatedly warns against this sin (Josh. 7:21; Rom. 7:7; 2 Peter 2:10)."[19]

These scriptures support the fact that God is against this practice and that it offends His holiness.

The American Dream may lead us into the spirit of greed which is an outgrowth of covetousness. *Psychology Today* states: "The greedy person is too attached to his things and his money, or he desires more money and more things in an excessive way. Greed has unpleasant effects on our inner emotional lives...."[20]

Many might agree that the spirit of greed is harmful. The Christian, however, must realize that our hopes, goals and dreams are to be fully influenced by the Holy Spirit. The article, "The American Dream vs. The Christian's Hope," by Melissa Kruger, describes where our sentiments should lie in our life and walk with Christ:

---

18   "Covetousness." *The Merriam-Webster Dictionary*. 11th Ed. 2004. Print.
19   Youngblood, Ronald F, F F. Bruce, and R K. Harrison. Nelson's New Illustrated Bible Dictionary. Nashville: T. Nelson, 1995. Print.
20   December 11, 2010.

"The American Dream might just be best summed up as a life of freedom, personal happiness, material comfort and lasting fulfillment (all nicely enclosed in a white picket fence). Hard work, long hours, and independence are woven into the fabric of our hopes as the means by which to procure this dream. At times I fear that we mistakenly substitute the American Dream for our expectation of the Christian life. If we just love Jesus enough, serve in the church nursery every week, study our Bibles with vigor and understand all the right theology, surely our lives will follow the pattern of our dreams.

To be sure, diligence and hard work are important components of the Christian life. Time in the Word and prayer are blessings that grow and encourage our faith. There is no greater subject of study than God and I expect to spend all of eternity delighting in knowing Him more intimately. All of these items are vital for the Christian, but too often we interchange the blessings of the Christian life with a vision of the American dream."[21]

Solomon's Code of Covetousness

King Solomon, as stated previously, certainly in our contemporary times would have experienced the best of the American Dream, and all that life had to offer. Yet he still hated his life and experienced a profound sense of covetousness when he considered his posterity in Ecclesiastes 2:18-19:

---

21   Kruger, Melissa. "The American Dream vs. The Christian's Hope." http://www.reformation21.org/blog/2014/09/the-american-dream-vs-the-chri.php. Sept. 8, 2014.

"Yea, I hated all my labour which I had taken under
the sun: because I should leave it unto the man that
shall be after me. And who knoweth whether he shall
be a wise man or a fool? yet shall he have rule over
all my labour wherein I have laboured, and wherein I havshewed myself wise under the sun. This is also
vanity."

Since the fall of Adam, each of us has worked by the sweat
of our brow, from sun-up to sundown, to secure and procure a livelihood and provision for our homes and families.
Yet what and who are we doing it all for? Solomon had a
profound sense of dissatisfaction when he considered the
disposition of his vast wealth and resources.

He confessed that he hated all his labour when he considered the prospect of leaving an inheritance to his children.
It is almost shocking that he stated this sentiment, when
we consider that he had stated previously in the proverbial
writings:

"A good man leaveth an inheritance to his children's
children: and the wealth of the sinner is laid up for
the just" (Proverbs 13:22).

Where did the change of mind and attitude come from?
We must remember that we are now examining the considerations of Solomon the aged, who had seen the apex of life
and the hearts of men, and concluded that "...all is vanity"
(Eccl. 1:2). This Solomon had experienced all life had to
offer, witnessed betrayal even in his own family, and he had
seen children disappoint their fathers.

Fathers typically seek to secure the provision of their

children after their demise, but after considering the character of his children and even humankind, Solomon became cynical, selfish and covetousness. He based his generosity and willingness to provide for and leave an inheritance to his children on their morality, worthiness, performance and their capacity to please him.

Yet the paradox is that he was particularly grieved by things he could never know that were completely out of his control. He mused in Ecclesiastes 2:19,

> "And who knoweth whether he shall be a wise man or a fool? yet shall he have rule over all my labour wherein I have laboured, and wherein I have shewed myself wise under the sun. This is also vanity."

He could never know in his life or in his grave that Rehoboam in his youthful folly would split his kingdom in 1 Kings 12. Perhaps the Lord had given him some insight which possibly incited his aggravation, but he could never be truly sure. Yet there he was, seeking to snatch the bread out his children's mouths, with a selfish eye and covetous hand. The thought of it aggravated him to no end. He was angered by the consideration that someone else, namely his children or the future king, would have rule over what he in his wisdom and industriousness produced. He felt that only he had the right to enjoy his material things. Like the pharoahs of Egypt, Solomon likely would not have been opposed to burying his wealth with him. As a result, he not only hated his life, but he also hated his work.

We read many contemporary stories of the wealthy who determine to make their children earn their inheritance, through some virtue, or by making them work their way to the top. Whether these efforts stem from covetousness, or a sober estimation of their children, one will never know. Yet this was Solomon's discontent as he considered his demise — one of covetousness.

How, then, does the Bible as a whole deal with the subject of covetousness? It is such a vast subject that weaves into so many other sinful acts that I am going to discuss two areas: Comparison and Competition.

The Crux of Comparison

Life's dreams and hopes many times can be based on comparison. There is a difference between good and bad, sweet and sour, up and down and weak and strong. We use measurements in every area of our lives to determine what is appropriate and what is unacceptable. When I go shopping for clothes, comparison plays a great part in my choices and considerations. *Is it too long or too short? Is it right for the occasion? Is it the right size? Is it the right price?* The whole shopping experience is based on comparing style with style, price with price, color with color and size with size. Therefore, comparison is not a terrible or unreasonable practice.

It, however, can become a weapon against spiritual and emotional health when used in the spirit of covetousness. The Apostle Paul addressed the folly of comparing in his epistle to the Corinthian church:

> "For we dare not make ourselves of the number, or compare ourselves with some that commend themselves: but they measuring themselves by themselves, and comparing themselves among themselves, are not wise" (2 Corinthians 10:12).

Let's look at a few passages of scripture that speak to this strong desire of wanting and seeking another's possession or position borne out of comparison. The first passage is found in Luke 12:13 (ASV):

"And one out of the multitude said unto him, Teacher, bid my brother divide the inheritance with me."

According to the laws of that culture, the oldest son would receive the greater of the inheritance in comparison to all the other sons. This is stated as such in Deuteronomy 21:17: "But he shall acknowledge the son of the hated for the firstborn, by giving him a double portion of all that he hath: for he is the beginning of his strength; the right of the firstborn is his." The execution of this law was dependent on the heart and mind of the individual. The older brother had to be just and righteous in order to give what is just and right to his brother(s). The younger brothers had to be satisfied and contented with their portion for them to receive their inheritance without the spirit of comparison.

Who is being covetous in this passage by comparing and withholding the rights of the other? It appears to be the older brother who seemingly is refusing to share or divide the portions justly. This behavior on the part of the older is an indication that he compared himself to his brother, by seeing himself as being entitled to all of the inheritance and refusing to acknowledge his brother as being deserving of any portion of it. When we think of ourselves as being better, superior, worthy or entitled, we are actually measuring or evaluating what is right for us or right for the other person.

This practice is prevalent in our hearts and lives and operates daily. For example, a person can be robbed of a promotion that they earned and deserved because their superiors think that it may be too good or prosperous for them. They compare the person's worth to themselves or to someone else that they feel is more valuable. We do not have to look far in our society, workplace, home and even in church to see that this practice is prevalent. Many souls are carrying around torches of hate, rejection, anxiety, insecurity, anger and disappointment because of how they were raised in a family that was based on comparison.

As a pastor, I have had to counsel many believers as they comb through their emotional puddles of resentment and despair. In many cases, it was noted that they grew up in large families where they had to share almost everything to survive. The sad saga of these stories is that within this survival mechanism, comparison played a key role.

I have heard stories from youngest siblings, who felt that they had to wear hand-me-downs, while older children had the newer clothes. Food was also a great issue in these families, especially when there was a scarcity at the table. I have heard adults lament that certain of their siblings always received larger portions than they. To this day, they are obsessed with food because of it, by overeating or withholding from their own family members. It sometimes leads to generational comparison, where the person who feels cheated may dote on one of their own children more than the other.

The Seduction of Social

Advancements in technology have created a profound sense of misery and anxiety in the hearts of many individuals. With the advent of the cell phone and social media sites like Facebook and Instagram, we can now see how much better our neighbors are doing than we are. A *Psychology Today* article notes:

> "...No matter how successful you are, you are (probably) not a billionaire. But you can see how billionaires live with the push of a button. You can see how the rich and famous go about their daily lives, what they have that you don't, how they live that you can't. The disparity is now transparent, and it pushes ancient psychological triggers we developed for important evolutionary reasons."[22]

Time Magazine declares:

> "On lifestyle-focused sites like Instagram, a user may see a friend's perfectly framed, glamorous photos and compare herself negatively to those images."[23]

It is the technological version of "Keeping Up With The Jones," which is the never-ending pursuit of maintaining the same standard of living as our neighbors. Yet the deception of the matter is that while we are in the heat of comparison, we only see the highlights, the glossy moments, and the "wins" in the lives of the people that we are envying. As we visually peruse and sample the carefully crafted lives of others, gratitude and thankfulness for what we have received from the Lord is wiped clean out of our hearts. When we

22   Hayes, Dr. Stephen C., "The Unexpected Way That New Technology Makes Us Unhappy." Psychology Today. Sept. 2, 2014. https://www.psychologytoday.com/us/blog/get-out-your-mind/201409/the-unexpected-way-new-technology-makes-us-unhappy.

23   Heid, M. "You Asked: Is Social Media Making Me Miserable?" Aug. 2, 2017. http://time.com/4882372/social-media-facebook-instagram-unhappy.

see our neighbors enjoying things that we think we ought to possess, we forget appreciation and embrace disappointment and despair. Because we see no easy way out of our circumstances, we end up hating our lives.

The act of comparison borne out of covetousness can lead us to extreme practices in our relationships, trying to dull the pain of disappointment. The classic book, *Aesop's Fables,* holds a timeless story worth sharing:

> "A woman possessed a Hen that gave her an egg every day. She often thought with herself how she might obtain two eggs daily instead of one, and at last, to gain her purpose, determined to give the Hen a double allowance of barley. From that day the Hen became fat and sleek, and never once laid another egg. Covetousness overreacheth itself."[24]

The Parable of the Real Prodigal

Another instance in the Bible that may bring more clarity to the subject of comparison and covetousness is the story of the prodigal son. Luke 15:11-32 gives us a great parable that speaks to many spiritual and moral issues of our lives.

I, however, would like to focus on the aspect of comparison and covetousness within the storyline of the parable of the prodigal. You probably know this story, but just to give an overview, I will relate some key portions. The younger son took his inheritance and went far away to live his life unscrupulously. He partied, and was wanton, excessive and riotous. This could be any of us or any of our children. They leave to go college, or to have their own apartment and then they become out of control because of the new-found free-

---

24   Aesop. (2007). *A Woman and Her Hen.* In D.L. Ashliman (Ed.), Aesop's Fables (pp. 246-247). New York: Penguin Group.

dom from parental or spiritual boundaries. I think most of us have had this experience on some level or another.

The consequence of living loosely is very costly and could be deadly. In this story the young man ended up in a pig's sty, eating what the pig refused, without friends and money. He woke out of his folly and decided to go back home, hoping that his father would receive him and give him whatever shelter or position he had left. The father surprised him by throwing him a great party, restoring him to his position of sonship and assuring him of his fatherly love.

The demonstration of comparison came from his elder brother, who issued out of the loins of the same father. This brother stayed at home, worked hard, obeyed his father and served diligently. When the younger brother came home, the whole house was filled with laughter and celebration. He heard the music, the merriment and the festivity. Instead of joining in, he had a violent, repulsive reaction. Here is his response to the return of his long-lost brother in Luke 15:26- 30:

> "And he called one of the servants, and asked what these things meant. And he said unto him, Thy brother is come; and thy father hath killed the fatted calf, because he hath received him safe and sound. And he was angry, and would not go in: therefore came his father out, and intreated him. And he answering said to his father, Lo, these many years do I serve thee, neither transgressed I at any time thy commandment: and yet thou never gavest me a kid, that I might make merry with my friends: But as soon as this thy son was come, which hath devoured thy living with harlots, thou hast killed for him the fatted calf."

The father was very concerned, because the older son had ignored the fact that he never lost anything while his brother was away, and he would lose nothing in his brother's return. The eldest compared himself as the model child to his brother and felt that the prodigal did not deserve the festive gathering, because he had made so many mistakes. Does this sound familiar, reader? Ultimately, the older brother was the real prodigal son. He had become so consumed with wanting more that he could not appreciate everything he always had. The father reminded him of this fact in Luke 15:31-32:

> "And he said unto him, Son, thou art ever with me, and all that I have is thine. It was meet that we should make merry, and be glad: for this thy brother was dead, and is alive again; and was lost, and is found."

In other words, the older son had all the father possessed and would always have it. There was no need to resent the portion that the younger brother received. Oh, that we would learn to just trust God for His plan and purpose for our lives! We would experience such rest and peace as we enjoy His presence and show love to our brothers and sisters.

His Enough Is Enough

The little ones around me that are always invading my privacy make demands on my life for my time, my space and my approval. Now I am not complaining, because they bring joy, laughter and challenge to my life. However, the constant cry among them is, "You never!" This means that I never give one the same as I gave to the other. To put a lid on this complaint, I usually tell them to make note of when "I always," whatever that always is. The issue is that they got something at some point, but in their childish minds, it was not enough. Hopefully, they will be taught and learn the principle of having God's enough. God, Who is the Creator and Sustainer of life, gives us what we need, what we are built to handle and where we are designed to go. The misery that we often feel is when we are not in agreement with His way, His Word and His purpose.

The next aspect of covetousness I would like to examine is the notion of competition. I can feel some of you getting tight right now, because many of us have been raised and nurtured in a society that glorifies competition. Whether it is in sports, academics, relationships and recreation, we are prone to think that the only way to make it is to compete. But first, allow me to share my personal experience journeying through covetous comparison.

The Comparison Quest: A Personal Testimony

I had been preaching for many years before 1989, when I was ordained. I traveled nationally and internationally preaching, teaching and doing workshops. The doors for ministry opened across denominational lines, which afforded me the privilege of ministering in different arenas.

My academic background was in the medical field, but I had no official theological training on the seminary level. My late pastor, Bishop Wilbert S. McKinley, was such a scholar and student of the Bible that he imparted his knowledge to his ministers freely. He goaded us to study and even taught us how to choose the right material for study. He constantly rehearsed the doctrines of the Church, the principles of Reformed theology and proper preparation for sermon delivery. He was intense and intentional when it came to the grooming of his leaders for ministry and service.

Yet, I felt insufficient when it came to the lack of a seminary degree. This feeling of incompleteness was fueled by my desire to be recognized by those who had degrees within my circle. I compared myself to the degreed ministers, not in an envious way, but in a comparative way. I really wanted to present myself to my audience as a credibly prepared minister of the Gospel. There was nothing wrong with seeking to improve and upgrade myself in ministry, but the motive is that I focused on others and not on what, when and how God wanted me to function in His Kingdom. The Lord continually through His Word confronted my restless spirit and constantly assured me that my calling and vocation was designed by Him and all I had to do was to follow His lead.

These words brought rest to my spirit and I continued to minister with the ability and preparation that He had afforded me. It was many years later that He opened the door for me to finish my preparation by attending and graduating from seminary. This experience was beyond my minute vision of myself and my calling. You see, I was concerned about seminary only to enhance my ministry and to become more credible based on comparison.

When I abandoned that quest and simply waited on God to guide me, His purpose became clearer and wider in my mind and spirit. Approximately two years after graduation, I was approached by another institution to open a Bible college through my church. One of the stipulations was that the president of such college must have a doctorate in ministry. It was then that it clicked in my mind that the degree was not about my preaching skill, or my credibility, but my availability to create opportunity for others to be prepared for their divine vocation.

I hope you can see what I received from my feeble experience of comparison. When we compare ourselves to others with the spirit of covetousness, we not only miss out on the bigger picture of God's eternal purpose for our lives, but for His purpose in the lives of others.

Please understand that there is certainly nothing wrong with admiring others who have done outstanding things in their lives. Do not confuse inspiration and admiration for the sin of covetous comparison. I have been inspired by many noble persons, but I also learned that their inspiration must bring me into God's realization. Philippians 1:6 says: "Being confident of this very thing, that he which hath begun a good work in you will perform it until the day of Jesus Christ."

Covetousness and Competition

The world of sports, entertainment, education, business and even relationships is built and sustained on the premise of who is going to be on top. When we look at game shows, we see that only the winner is celebrated and given a special prize and offered special laudation. We often witness individuals doing unscrupulous, unprincipled things to ensure that they win. Many of our children participate in sports and the driving force many times is that the child becomes a winner, not that the child enjoys the sport or plays fairly and by the rules.

Livestrong.com published an article, "Negatives of Competitive Sports," which speaks about children, but can also be applied to adults.

"Participation in competitive sports has long been a staple of high school culture. Not only does it help kids stay in shape, learn focus and socialize, but it also teaches them about working under pressure. Competition is about challenging yourself to improve. But the world of competitive sports also has a negative side. If not monitored, competitive sports can harm athletes physiologically, socially and physically...."

The author goes on to say:

"Competitive sports improve athletic skill and teach players how to work with teammates and win, which can be helpful lessons. When the focus shifts from athleticism to winning, however, what was once an enjoyable and supportive activity can turn into a high-pressure and anxiety-filled job for a child. The mounting pressure to play well can increase stress and make children feel bad and lose confidence should they make mistakes or lose. Even players who win most of the time may lose the pleasure of participating because of the pressure they place on themselves."[25]

It is the same in all areas of competition. This negative competition is fueled by the spirit and drive of covetousness. People want adulation and admiration to follow their achievements. Yet the writer of this article states that it can lead to the development of a poor attitude. The author goes on to declare:

---

25 Huggins, T. Marice. https://www.livestrong.com/article/523284-nega-tives-of-competitive-sports.

"Winning is always one of the main objectives of sports competitions. Coaches spend tremendous amounts of time perfecting drills and shaping their plays to give players a competitive edge. If not monitored, the drive to win can soon change to a win-at-all-costs mentality that can lead to attitude problems. The attitude that you must win can encourage cheating and difficulty getting along with others on and off the field."[26]

This writer has opened for us the need to examine our quest, even as believers, to always win at any cost in church and outside of our church activities.

Is Competition Biblical?

What does the Bible say about competition? First, what does this word mean? "Competition," according to the *Oxford English Dictionary*, means "the activity or condition of striving to gain or win something by defeating or establishing superiority over others."[27] Please be reminded that competition is part and parcel of our capitalistic system in a democratic society. It is seen on all levels of our trafficking. As mentioned before, it encourages people to strive for their best; it gives the community an opportunity to choose and hopefully brings out creativity and originality in competitors' areas of interest.

It becomes toxic, however, when covetousness accompanies the spirit of competitiveness. This combination can be lethal and will attack unity, respect, honor and growth in a

---

26   Ibid.

27   Simpson, J A, and E S. C. Weiner. *The Oxford English Dictionary*. Oxford: Clarendon Press, 1989. Print.

Christian context. We are not entities unto ourselves. Because we have been purposed to grow and work together, this way of thinking and living is dangerous to the Body of Christ.

On his podcast, Dr. Steve Greene addressed the subject, "Competition Brings Division in the Body of Christ," stating:

> "Did you know there is a very common word that is used in our culture that you cannot find in the Bible? It is the word 'competition.' Jesus never talked about it, but He did talk about the opposite of that word.
>
> "The greatest power God's children have over darkness is unity. Jesus talked a great deal about His oneness with the Father and the importance of unity in the Body of Christ. It is the most difficult command Jesus gave to the Church because it wars against the most evil aspect of our sin nature—independence.
>
> "The walls of division and competition among His Body are a stench in God's nostrils. He sees the competition and the pride of ownership and weeps for the lost who cannot come to Him because they cannot see Him in His Body. When His Body is one, the unbelieving see that Jesus was sent by God. It is like a supernatural key that unlocks heaven for the heathen soul. The key is in the hand of Christ's Church. When there is unity, there is power..."[28]

Bringing The Flesh Under

How, then, could the Bible be against competition when the Apostle Paul uses so many terms that suggest rivalry, race and contest? Let us look at 1 Corinthians 9:24-27:

---

28   drstevegreene.com/podcasts. August 22, 2013.

"Know ye not that they which run in a race run all, but one receiveth the prize? And every man that striveth for the mastery is temperate in all things. Now they do it to obtain a corruptible crown; but we an incorruptible. I therefore so run, not as uncertainly; so fight I, not as one that beateth the air: But I keep under my body, and bring it into subjection: lest that by any means, when I have preached to others, I myself should be a castaway."

These terms were not used to stress competition, but discipline. Paul alluded to the imagery of athletes preparing for the Olympic games, which required strenuous exercises, a sacrificial lifestyle and intentional self-denial. He then used this comparison to instruct us how to use the same applications of striving, fighting, and running to show that these disciplines helped the athlete to win. Therefore, if we pray, read the Bible, engage in fasting, and obey the Lord with the same vigor and vitality, we will overcome and become more and more like the Lord Jesus. This does not suggest competing with each other in the Body of Christ. It is speaking about bringing our flesh under the influence of the Holy Spirit for His glory.

The same Apostle Paul speaks to us about the Body of Christ and its function in the Kingdom. He describes the Body's function as equal to the function of the human body. The way our nerves, bones, tissue, muscles, organs and vessels work together to cause us to function as a whole is the same way the Church should operate so that it can be alive.

"From whom the whole body fitly joined together and compacted by that which every joint supplieth, according to the effectual working in the measure of every part, maketh increase of the body unto the edifying of itself in love" (Ephesians 4:16).

This concept will not work if the joints are fighting and resisting each other. The Bible says that we are many members, but one Body. One cannot say that the other is not needed or important. Therefore, there is no competing or outdoing of any member, if the Body is to function in a healthy manner.

Say Yes to Contentment

The question arises: *How can we ward off the spirit of covetousness that lurks in all of our hearts and minds daily?*

Alistair Begg declares,

> "If we are to say no to covetousness, we must learn to say yes to contentment. This involves learning to be content with what we have (Hebrews 13:5). Much of our discontentment may be traced to expectations that are essentially selfish and more often than not completely unrealistic."[29]

In the Ten Commandments, God clearly states in Exodus 20:17:

> "Thou shalt not covet thy neighbour's house, thou shalt not covet thy neighbour's wife, nor his manservant, nor his maidservant, nor his ox, nor his ass, nor any thing that is thy neighbour's."

This command from God deals with the propensity of the human heart to be terribly self-centered. The purpose of

---

29   Begg, Alistair. *Pathway to Freedom: How God's Law Guides Our Lives.* Chicago, IL: Moody Publishers. 2003. p. 215.

covetousness is to gratify the one and only, which is one-self. It is so consumed with that desire that no one else and nothing else matters. It will stop at nothing, which often includes the acts of stealing, lying and killing to get what it wants. Yes, the spirit of covetousness is strong, passionate, driven and insatiable.

The Folly of Covetousness

This insatiable appetite can be readily seen in the discourse that Jesus had with His disciples which was illustrated by a story about a farmer as stated in Luke 12:15:

> "And he said unto them, Take heed, and beware of covetousness: for a man's life consisteth not in the abundance of the things which he possesseth."

From the 16th to the 21st verse, Jesus shared a parable, which is an earthly illustration with a spiritual message. The parable was about a rich man who was a successful farmer. He reaped an abundant harvest and had to build another barn to accommodate his abundance. He told his soul to indulge by eating, drinking and being merry. He took complete satisfaction in himself and his gatherings. He delighted in his "stuff" and forgot about his soul, the only eternal part of him. That night his soul was called back to his Maker (God) and he had to leave all his "stuff" behind.

> "But God said unto him, Thou fool, this night thy soul shall be required of thee: then whose shall those things be, which thou hast provided? So is he that layeth up treasure for himself, and is not rich toward God" (Luke 12:20-21).

One of the key words in this story is "abundance." The Greek word for "abundance" in this text is *perisseuo* (per-is-syoo'-o;) which means "excess or surplus or over and above what one has, what one needs." Never satisfied, covetousness is constantly drawn to something better, prettier, nicer, richer, stronger and even nobler. Even doing what is seemingly good can be done out of a covetous heart.

Jesus gave the solution to this driving force that often causes us to be swallowed up with selfish desires in Luke 12:15:

> "And he said unto them, Take heed, and beware of covetousness: for a man's life consisteth not in the abundance of the things which he possesseth."

We should not measure ourselves by what we have or gain. We are more important than what we wear, where we live and what we accomplish. It does not mean that we should not be concerned about the necessities of life, but we should not value ourselves by them or the lack of them.

How, then, should we put a check on greed, dissatisfaction and discontentment? What must we do to quell the desire for abundance and plenty? Jesus gave the answer in the same chapter in Verses 30-32:

> "For all these things do the nations of the world seek after: and your Father knoweth that ye have need of these things; But rather seek ye the kingdom of God; and all these things shall be added unto you. Fear not, little flock; for it is your Father's good pleasure to give you the kingdom."

Jesus wants to be the center of our desires, wishes and needs. If we put Him first, trust and obey Him, we will have a satisfied soul and contentment will rule our hearts and minds. With Him, there is little room for fear, anxiety and hopelessness, which are emotions that fuel the need to want more, and compete and compare ourselves with others. Trusting God daily will calm our fears and assure us of His care and provision. Fanny Crosby's beloved hymn, "What a Friend We Have in Jesus," declares:

> *O what peace we often forfeit,*
> *O what needless pain we bear.*
> *All because we do not carry*
> *Everything to God in prayer.*

Stop right now and give your ambitions, passions and desires to the Lord. Let us ask Him to put His finger on anything that would cause us to want what we want at any cost. He will provide and His provision will sustain us.

CHAPTER FOUR

Pride & Rebellion

I AM DOING IT MY WAY

P RIDE. GONE are the days when pride is considered a bad thing. In our world today, the word "pride" has rid itself of all negative connotations and now evokes a sense of uniqueness and dignity. Pride has, in a contemporary sense, become attached to many different causes and interest groups. Whether black pride, white pride, gay pride or cultural pride, the secular world champions the concept that every individual should feel entitled to be who and what they are without shame or apology. In fact, they should be celebrated.

Pride is now designed to promote a sense of satisfaction, value, importance and distinction to the promoters of their cause. To present this word as detrimental or harmful in today's society would likely evoke strong opposition, because people enjoy the feeling of strength and affirmation that having pride brings. The Christian, however, cannot gravitate to the world's view on any subject, but must retain and guard the Bible's view.

So reader, although you may be proud about your identity, physical appearance, accomplishments, pedigree, spirituality or anything that you deem special, we still have to examine what the Bible says about this word and how it relates to our walk with God and each other.

The word "pride" is laced throughout the Old and the New Testaments and is mentioned 46 times in the King James Version of the Bible. The Hebrew form of pride is *ga'ah* OT:1342, which means "to be proud, be exalted."[30]

This word, however, when used to describe people, is associated with arrogance, evil behavior, obstinate speech and an insolent attitude. It is used to describe the opposite of humility.

In the New Testament, the Greek words for pride are *alazonia, huperephania,* and *tuphoo* NT:5187, which is to be "puffed up." These words can also indicate that which is "boastful, high minded and haughty." One Bible dictionary declares:

> "Pride is inordinate and unreasonable self-esteem, attended with insolence and rude treatment of others. Pride manifests itself by praising ourselves, adoring our persons, attempting to appear before others in a superior light to what we are; contempt and slander of others; envy at the excellences others possess; anxiety to gain applause; distress and rage when slighted; impatience of contradiction, and opposition to God himself."[31]

These definitions and connotations are a far cry from how society wants us to apply this word to our daily lives. But where and when did this word come into the life of human existence?

---

30   Strong, James. Strong's Exhaustive Concordance of the Bible. Abingdon Press, 1890. Print.

31   McClintock and Strong Encyclopedia, Electronic Database. © 2000 by Biblesoft.

The Practice of Pride

> "And the serpent said unto the woman, Ye shall not surely die: For God doth know that in the day ye eat thereof, then your eyes shall be opened, and ye shall be as gods, knowing good and evil. And when the woman saw that the tree was good for food, and that it was pleasant to the eyes, and a tree to be desired to make one wise, she took of the fruit thereof, and did eat, and gave also unto her husband with her; and he did eat" (Genesis 3:5-7).

This passage does not have the word "pride" mentioned, but the practice of pride was laced throughout the conversation, the decision and the experience. The enemy's main purpose was to oppose the will of God for mankind by exalting and promoting their minds to be equal with God. Pride is to lift ourselves above the exaltation and recognition of God. This passage shows us that the rejection of total dependency on God creates a need for total dependency on ourselves.

In our modern vernacular, the popular terms to describe the cry for freedom and independence are "autonomy" and "agency." You see, in the Garden of Eden, God was the Supreme Authority. He did not consult anyone concerning any matters. He did not create Adam from the dust, breathe into him, and when he became alive, ask him if he would like to change his identity. Adam was created in the image and likeness of God:

> "And God said, Let us make man in our image, after our likeness: and let them have dominion over the fish of the sea, and over the fowl of the air, and over the

cattle, and over all the earth, and over every creeping thing that creepeth upon the earth" (Gen. 1:26).

The Lord formed man out of the dust of the earth. The word formed in the Hebrew is from the *Strong's Concordance* OT:3335, which is *yatsar* (yaw-tsar'), meaning to squeeze into shape or to mold into form, to fashion or frame as the potter does the clay.[32] The sovereign God determined what man should look like, where he should live and what he should be doing. He also determined his companion.

> "And the Lord God said, It is not good that the man should be alone; I will make him an help meet for him. And out of the ground the Lord God formed every beast of the field, and every fowl of the air; and brought them unto Adam to see what he would call them: and whatsoever Adam called every living creature, that was the name thereof. And Adam gave names to all cattle, and to the fowl of the air, and to every beast of the field; but for Adam there was not found an help meet for him. And the Lord God caused a deep sleep to fall upon Adam and he slept: and he took one of his ribs, and closed up the flesh instead thereof; And the rib, which the Lord God had taken from man, made he a woman, and brought her unto the man. And Adam said, This is now bone of my bones, and flesh of my flesh: she shall be called Woman, because she was taken out of Man. Therefore shall a man leave his father and his mother, and shall cleave unto his wife: and they shall be one flesh. And

32   Strong, James. Strong's Exhaustive Concordance of the Bible. Abingdon Press, 1890. Print.

they were both naked, the man and his wife, and were not ashamed" (Genesis 2:18-25).

This scripture tells us that God made Eve and presented her to Adam and Adam recognized her and accepted her as the only choice for him. She also did not question her appearance and identity, because the God of the ages formed her for His purpose and her benefit.

In Eden, they were also given their assignment to take charge, supervise the animals, and tend the Garden. Their assignment was given to them without their requesting it. Everything that they were, everything that they had, and everything that they had to do was given to them by the Supreme Authority, Jehovah God. Along with the freedom to enjoy and rule their environment, there was one prohibition — to never eat of the tree of the knowledge of good and evil. The one and only "do not" was a caution to keep them from having to intimately know and experience evil — its burden, power and consequence. They were told that if they ate of this tree, they would surely die. This was clear and concise instruction from their Creator. Because of this, to disrupt this fellowship of agreement between God, Adam and Eve, the enemy had to downplay the seriousness of the prohibition. He sought to confuse Eve and minimize the import and intent of God's command. The enemy had to make them feel that the devastating consequence did not apply to their deceived action. So it is with us today.

Consequences of Autonomy

Let's look at an epidemic that has aggressively and rapidly taken over our communities, affecting believers as well as non-believers; adults as well as children; rich as well as poor, and white as well as non-white — the Opioid Epidemic. The National Institute of Drug Abuse wrote:

> "Every day, more than 130 people in the United States die after overdosing on opioids. The misuse of and addiction to opioids—including prescription pain relievers, heroin, and synthetic opioids such as fentanyl—is a serious national crisis that affects public health as well as social and economic welfare. The Centers for Disease Control and Prevention estimates that the total "economic burden" of prescription opioid misuse alone in the United States is $78.5 billion a year, including the costs of healthcare, lost productivity, addiction treatment, and criminal justice involvement."[33]

This dire situation has caught the attention of politicians and some attempt is being made to rectify this plaque. This crisis did not just happen outside of the fact that sin brings consequences. Just as Adam and Eve violated God's command and were subject to physical, emotional and spiritual destruction, so is our society which thrives on its autonomy being subjected to the tragedy of its choices.

Believers are also suffering from wanting to do their own thing apart from the dictates of God's divine will. What is autonomy? *Merriam-Webster* defines *autonomy* as "self-directing freedom and especially moral independence personal autonomy; a self-governing state." In other words, I am in control of my life, my decisions and my destiny. Adam and Eve didn't bargain for this when they were introduced to the notion of being their own god, being

---

equal to God and doing things their own way. The result is that we are caught up in the world of self-centeredness and self-deception. This legacy is what Adam and Eve passed on to us. We are convinced that we can do it our way, without God, and be happy and complete.

Paul Tripp, president of Paul Tripp Ministries, wrote an article entitled "You're Fooling Yourself." He describes for us one of the destructive tendencies that we exhibit when we exercise our independence from the authority of God. He describes the "Foolishness of Self-sufficiency" saying:

> "We're all very good at making ourselves feel good about what God says is bad. We're all very skilled at recasting what we've done so what was wrong doesn't look so wrong to us. I'll tell myself that I didn't really lash out in anger; no, I was speaking as one of God's prophets. I'll tell myself that the second look wasn't lust; I am simply a man who enjoys beauty. I'll tell myself that I'm not craving power; I'm just exercising God-given leadership gifts.
>
> "Foolishness is able to do something dangerous. It's able to look at wrong and see right. Had David been able to see himself with accuracy and if he'd been able to see his sin for what it really was, it's hard to imagine that he would have continued to travel down that pathway."[34]

We are no different from Adam, Eve and David because we want to do things our way. We are driven to live according to our rules and ignore any restriction on what we feel, want and like.

---

34 https://www.desiringgod.org/articles/youre-fooling-yourself. Nov 17, 2010.

Ignoring the Consequences

I remember when I lived in Brooklyn, New York, and worked at Harlem Hospital in Manhattan. In Brooklyn, there are very few parking spaces where you can just leave your car without worrying, due to extremely strict parking rules. On certain days, you had to move your car to the other side of the street at a certain time or risk the consequences. I was young and full of myself, believing that those rules did not apply to me and my car. I would jump up in the mornings to drive for 45 minutes from Brooklyn to Harlem, ignoring the parking ticket that was placed on the windshield of my car.

This went on for a long time, with me thinking that I could just put the accumulating tickets away and nothing would happen to me. I created my own law, with the excuse that I work very hard and have to drive a distance to work; therefore, special rules should be made for me and my slothfulness. Well, needless to say, this ignorant, foolish way of thinking cost me my license. I went through a period of great embarrassment and discomfort because I received a restricted license and had to pay a large bill to clean it up in order to regain my full driver's license. Yes, I was convinced that it was not a major crime and it was not that serious, until consequences kicked in. I am sure you have your own stories of how self-sufficiency, autonomy and self-deception can carve out a great price to pay. Sin is still reigning in the earth and in our lives because of Adam and Eve.

A Portrait of Pride

By now you should be able to see how pride is the mother of it all. Yes, pride rules the areas of self-centeredness, self-sufficiency and self-righteousness.

What does self-centeredness look like in the Bible? There was a man named Nabal [NAY bal] whose name means "empty person." He was a very wealthy sheep-master. You can read the story in 1 Samuel 25. David had an army of six hundred men that had served as protectors for Nabal's shepherds and flocks against the Bedouin Arabs. David asked Nabal for bread and water, since David and his men were living as fugitives, trying to survive the harshness of the time and King Saul's pursuit. However, Nabal was cruel, mean and self-centered. He disregarded the kindness that David and his men extended him at the peril of their lives. He answered by saying:

> "...Who is David? and who is the son of Jesse? there be many servants now a days that break away every man from his master. Shall I then take my bread, and my water, and my flesh that I have killed for my shearers, and give it unto men, whom I know not whence they be?" (1 Sam. 25:10-11).

Nabal wanted to cover His covetousness and selfishness by degrading David with accusations of unjust behavior towards Saul, and depriving David of food and care, which was based on his selfishness. David became irate and distraught, declaring that he would retaliate by killing Nabal and all the men in his camp. David went into a self-protective mode against Nabal's verbal assaults and planned to attack Nabal because of his self-centered response to him. David was about to get his hands pretty dirty just before he would become King of Israel. However, Abigail, Nabal's wife, interceded and quieted David's rage so that blood would not be shed, and David would not be swallowed up by Nabal's ill-fated disposition. She reached out to David to prevent his rage:

> "And when Abigail saw David, she hasted, and lighted off the ass, and fell before David on her face, and bowed herself to the ground, And fell at his feet, and said, Upon me, my lord, upon me let this iniquity be: and let thine handmaid, I pray thee, speak in thine audience, and hear the words of thine handmaid. Let not my lord, I pray thee, regard this man of Belial, even Nabal: for as his name is, so is he; Nabal is his name, and folly is with him: but I thine handmaid saw not the young men of my lord, whom thou didst send. Now therefore, my lord, as the Lord liveth, and as thy soul liveth, seeing the Lord hath withholden thee from coming to shed blood, and from avenging thyself with thine own hand, now let thine enemies, and they that seek evil to my lord, be as Nabal" (1 Sam. 25:23-25).

Abigail described her husband as being "a son of Belial" — which Bible dictionaries define as "worthless, a rebel, a rogue or a scoundrel." She also stated that her husband was a man of folly. This means he was a fool. In our contemporary language, we often use this term to connote someone's stupidity or ineptness. But in the Bible, being a fool does not mean that the person does not think, it means they think wrongly and rebelliously. They resort to their own wisdom and disregard the wisdom and truth of God. Psalm 14:1 says:

> "The fool hath said in his heart, There is no God. They are corrupt, they have done abominable works, there is none that doeth good."

If there is no God, then the person becomes the supreme authority of their lives. As their own supreme authority, they can do it their way without accountability to anyone. This, readers, is what self-centeredness really means.

The Myth of Self-Sufficiency

Another aspect of "doing things our way," is **self-sufficiency.** To understand this concept, we have to examine sufficiency. What does it mean? One dictionary defines "sufficiency" as "an amount of something that is enough, or the quality of being good enough." In Paul Tripp's article, in the portion of the article, "The Foolishness of Self-Sufficiency," he states:

> "We all like to think of ourselves as more independently capable than we actually are. We weren't created to be independent, autonomous, or self-sufficient. We were made to live in a humble, worshipful, and loving dependency upon God and in a loving and humble interdependency with others.
>
> "Our lives were designed to be community projects. Yet, the foolishness of sin tells us that we have all that we need within ourselves. So we settle for relationships that never go beneath the casual. We defend ourselves when the people around us point out a weakness or a wrong. We hold our struggles within, not taking advantage of the resources that God has given us.
>
> "The lie of the garden was that Adam and Eve could be like God, independent and self-sufficient. We still tend to buy into that lie."[35]

35   Tripp, Paul. https://www.desiringgod.org/articles/youre-fooling-yourself. Nov. 17, 2010.

Not by Might...

I bring your attention to the account in Scripture in the fourth chapter of the Book of Zechariah, where Zerubbabel was encouraged by the Lord to build a temple in Jerusalem for the returning captives coming out of Babylonian captivity. This was a very demanding task to accomplish, seeing that Jerusalem was completely sacked by the Babylonians and the temple that Solomon built was now demolished.

It was equally difficult to arouse the people to continue to build. They started out by building the altar but became discouraged and self-centered. They turned their hearts towards building their own homes and forgot the house of the Lord.

You see, the temple would become the place to restore worship, instruction, fellowship and guidance to a community that was scattered. They were returning with a new generation who needed to become entrenched in their religious tradition. It was not just a physical building that was needed. It was the rebuilding of a nation upon the truth of God's Word. It was restoring a people to their covenant relationship with their God.

The other hindrance to the building of the temple came from outside pressure, criticism and conflict.

> "After rebuilding the Temple foundation the first two years, construction came to a standstill for 17 years. This delay came principally because of opposition from settlers in Samaria who wanted to help with the building (Ezra 4:1-2). When the offer was refused because of the Samaritans' association with heathen worship, the Samaritans disrupted the building project (Ezra 4:4). Counselors were hired who misrepre-

sented the captives in court (Ezra 4:5), causing the Persian king to withdraw his support (Ezra 4:21). The delay in building also was due to the preoccupation of Zerubbabel and other captives with building houses for themselves (Hag 1:2-4)."[36]

This recorded series of interruptions laid the foundation for God to send the prophet Haggai to stir Zerubbabel to rise and accomplish his assignment. God spoke to him saying: "This is the word of the LORD unto Zerubbabel, saying, Not by might, nor by power, but by my spirit, saith the LORD of hosts" (Zechariah 4:6). This was a clear word against self-sufficiency. In other words, this task, with all its opposition, could not be accomplished with mere human effort.

Let's look at the tools of self-sufficiency that we use to get our job done our way. The first prohibition to the prophet was "not by might," which means, according to *Strong's Bible Concordance*, not by *chayil* (khah'-yil); from OT:2342; which means "force, whether of men, means or other resources; an army, wealth, virtue, valor, strength."[37] How many times have we had resources and financial connections, but the project did not get off the ground? Our success is not dependent on wealth or resources, even though we need wealth and resources. It simply means that our wealth or financial resources should not get the credit for anything that we have accomplished. The wealth itself comes from the Lord. The Bible states in Deuteronomy 8:18:

> "But thou shalt remember the Lord thy God: for it is he that giveth thee power to get wealth , that he may

---

36   Nelson's Illustrated Bible Dictionary, ©1986, Thomas Nelson Publishers.
37   Strong, James. Strong's Exhaustive Concordance of the Bible. Abingdon Press, 1890. Print.

establish his covenant which he sware unto thy fathers, as it is this day."

The next prohibitive word was that the prophet should
not attempt this task by his "power" — or anyone else's.
This word has to do with "physical or brute strength."
Most dictionaries declare that it means "force, strength or
physical ability." It is the same word used to describe the
strength that Samson had in his hair. Samson told Delilah
in Judges 16:17:

> "...That he told her all his heart, and said unto her,
> There hath not come a razor upon mine head;
> for I have been a Nazarite unto God from my mother's
> womb: if I be shaven, then my strength will go from
> me, and I shall become weak, and be like any other
> man."

The strength that he had caused him to fight victoriously
against any enemy. But when Samson's hair was gone, his
strength failed. The prophet was admonished not to rely on
physical strength or even mental power, because sickness
or unexpected circumstances often change or compromise
our abilities.

Finally, the prophet was told that the only way to avoid
self-sufficiency was to depend on the enabling of God's
Spirit. The encouragement was that His Spirit was sufficient to empower him to finish the task.

The Ruse of Self-Righteousness

The other debilitating force that hinders the Bible-believ-
ing Christian from advancing in the Faith is **self-righteous-**

ness. This is a strong weapon against one's growth and development in the character of Christ. This behavior causes one to believe that they can be good, right, and honorable without Christ, the Righteous One in their life. Righteousness, according to *Nelson's Bible Dictionary,* means "upright living or straightness according to God's standard." The Old Testament's account of the shedding of blood on God's altars and the New Testament's account of Jesus shedding of His Blood on the Cross declare that man's righteousness was not sufficient. From the Fall in the Garden of Eden, Adam and Eve caused us to inherit a nature that is unrighteous and corrupt. The prophet Isaiah noted in Isaiah 64:6:

> "But we are all as an unclean thing, and all our righteousnesses are as filthy rags; and we all do fade as a leaf; and our iniquities, like the wind, have taken us away."

This means we need to get our righteousness from outside of ourselves. Jesus hung on the Cross as the Righteous Seed so that if we receive Him as our Savior and believe that He is alive, His righteousness will be transferred to us. This amazing transaction is what has allowed us to stand in the presence of God, completely accepted by Him as His legal child, because of His Son's righteousness in us.

The term "pharisaical" connotes one who is religious and is also very self-righteous. The Pharisees were a religious group that adhered strictly to the Mosaic Law and all the other ceremonial laws that they deemed necessary to be good enough for God. They tried to impose these laws on others and if the others did not obey, they looked upon them as being unworthy of God's love and salvation. The

Scripture supports this by saying in Luke 18:9-14:

> "And he spake this parable unto certain which trusted
> in themselves that they were righteous, and despised
> others: Two men went up into the temple to pray; the
> one a Pharisee, and the other a publican. The Pharisee
> stood and prayed thus with himself, God, I thank thee,
> that I am not as other men are, extortioners, unjust,
> adulterers, or even as this publican. I fast twice in the
> week, I give tithes of all that I possess. And the publi-
> can, standing afar off, would not lift up so much as his
> eyes unto heaven, but smote upon his breast, saying,
> God be merciful to me a sinner. I tell you, this man
> went down to his house justified rather than the oth-
> er: for every one that exalteth himself shall be abased;
> and he that humbleth himself shall be exalted."

This text tells us how the Lord Jesus felt about religious, self-righteous people. We as believers sometimes forget that we all were born sinners, shapen in our mother's womb in iniquity and were naturally hostile to God and His holiness. There are times when we think that our morality, pedigree, education, profession and social standing make us more acceptable in the eyes of God than those who are not in the same circle. It is the mercy and love of God that drew us to Him. The grace that He afforded to us by the death of Jesus on the Cross gives us right standing. It is not good works, good behavior or a good life that will make us righteous in the sight of God. There is none good, but Him. Paul Tripp writes:

> "Why don't we celebrate grace more? Why aren't we
> more amazed by the wonderful gifts that are ours as

the children of God? Why don't we live with a deep sense of need, coupled with a deep sense of gratitude for how each need has been met by God's grace? Well, the answer is clear. You'll never celebrate grace as much as you should when you think you're more righteous than you actually are.

"Grace is the plea of sinners. Mercy is the hope of the wicked. Acceptance is the prayer of those who know that they could never do anything to earn it. But the foolishness of sin makes me righteous in my own eyes."[38]

The publican in the passage above shows the only way to walk in the righteousness of God and live straight and in right standing with the Father. Man is to accept the fact that we need the Righteousness of Jesus Christ.   How can you and I guard ourselves from self-centeredness, self-sufficiency and self-righteousness, which lead to the boastful declaration that "I did it my way"? We need to grow in grace and in the knowledge of the Lord Jesus Christ so that we can drown out ungodly propensities. The Word of God is the only way to fill our hearts with His way and His will.

I became the caregiver of my elderly parents. My father lived to be 90 and my mother lived to be 105. They both lived with me and required 24-hour care. This was a great challenge to me as a single woman, a traveling evangelist, and later a pastor with a growing congregation. How do I do this without panicking or falling apart? There were times when I felt that I could run things by organizing, planning and executing. Whenever I tried to do it on my own, I failed.

---

38 Tripp, Paul. "Psalm 51: Reductionism." https://www.christianity.com/blogs/paul-tripp/psalm-51-reductionism.html.

But, when I followed God, He sent help and gave me instruction; He gave me information and He gave me the grace to do. They both went home to be with the Lord, and I learned how to trust the Lord fully all the way to the end. It was a trying time, but it was not by might nor by power, but by the Spirit of the Lord (Zech. 4:6).

Please put aside your "ownwayness" and trust the Lord to show you His way. Here are some Bible verses that will help to keep you in check:

> Not that we are sufficient of ourselves to think anything as of ourselves; but our sufficiency is of God (2 Corinthians 3:5).

> I am the vine, ye are the branches: He that abideth in me, and I in him, the same bringeth forth much fruit: for without me ye can do nothing (John 15:5).

> But we have this treasure in earthen vessels, that the excellency of the power may be of God, and not of us. (1 Corinthians 15:10).

> But by the grace of God I am what I am: and his grace which was bestowed upon me was not in vain; but I laboured more abundantly than they all: yet not I, but the grace of God which was with me (2 Corinthians 4:7).

> For it is God which worketh in you both to will and to do of his good pleasure (Philippians 2:13).

> I can do all things through Christ which strengtheneth me (Philippians 4:13).

CHAPTER FIVE

The Sovereignty of God

THE ALL-KNOWING, ALL-POWERFUL, EVER-PRESENT GOD

I ASKED, "LORD, what does this mean? Why? Why would I be angry? Why would I be cowardly? Why would I be sad? Why would I be envious, disgusted and afraid? And just in general, why would I be offended?" And the Holy Spirit said that it's discontentment. And the anger was the first layer that He had for me. So the anger is that I'm not necessarily angry with you, but I'm angry at God. Because He has put me in this situation where it is not what I planned. This is not the life that I wanted. And this is not where I wanted to be. And so my anger is really at God. But because I can't do anything to God, I can't fight God, I'm going to fight you. That whole cowardly piece is not because I'm cowardly. It's just because I don't want to do it. I don't want to do it because it is not what I planned to do. Or what I wanted to be in my plans. - C.A.B.

In the previous chapter, I talked about our human propensity to do things our way, and disregard the voice and plan of God. Whether our choices in any matter were done ignorantly or willfully, it still speaks of a natural resistance to authority. In this chapter, however, I ask you to examine, grapple with and hopefully resolve the notion that God is our Supreme Authority, which means He was, is and always will be in charge.

This idea can be very disconcerting to human thought and can stir up very negative feelings towards any authoritative figure or absolute standard. It can be easy to feel that we must have the last say and we must be free to do as we feel. This thought, however, is contrary to the teachings of the Bible. Proverbs 3:5-7 states:

> "Trust in the Lord with all thine heart; and lean not unto thine own understanding. In all thy ways acknowledge him, and he shall direct thy paths. Be not wise in thine own eyes: fear the Lord, and depart from evil."

This passage teaches us that we must have confidence, hope and trust in the Lord, Jehovah the Self-existent God. This trust can be described as one running to God for refuge, covering and protection. This trust cannot be half-hearted, but it must be with our whole heart. The heart includes our emotions, intellect and will. All that we are should surrender itself to the God Who is sovereign. If we trust Him this way, then we will not be so quick to lean or support ourselves with and by our wisdom, tradition, experience, education and will. Instead, we will thrust ourselves solely upon the Word and will of God. But how do we do this?

First, everything we desire, think or do should be based on direction of the Lord, according to Verse 6. Acknowledging the Lord in our every move will guarantee His divine guidance. When we acknowledge or recognize God, it means to fully accept Him as the all-seeing, all-knowing and ever-present God that He is. This response will afford us the assurance that He will guide us in the path that He has chosen for us, which will bring glory and honor to His Name.

Understanding Sovereignty

He is sovereign, and maybe we're angry that He's sovereign. - J.O.E.

Before we continue this examination, it is important that we define the word "sovereignty." Most dictionaries state that it means "supreme power or authority." Theologically, it is His power and right of dominion over His creatures, to dispose and determine them as seems good to Him. This characteristic of God is demonstrated in His acts of creation, providence, and grace. His rule is also seen as universal, absolute and everlasting. Let us look at Daniel 4:34-37, where Nebuchadnezzar was forced to acknowledge a King greater than himself:

> "And at the end of the days I Nebuchadnezzar lifted up mine eyes unto heaven, and mine understanding returned unto me, and I blessed the most High, and I praised and honoured him that liveth forever, whose dominion is an everlasting dominion, and his kingdom is from generation to generation: And all the inhabitants of the earth are reputed as nothing: and he doeth according to his will in the army of heaven, and among the inhabitants of the earth: and none can stay his hand, or say unto him, What doest thou? At the same time my reason returned unto me; and for the glory of my kingdom, mine honour and brightness returned unto me; and my counsellors and my lords sought unto me; and I was established in my

kingdom, and excellent majesty was added unto me. Now I Nebuchadnezzar praise and extol and honour the King of heaven, all whose works are truth, and his ways judgment: and those that walk in pride he is able to abase."

We should also consider Paul's insights in Ephesians 1:3-12:

"Blessed be the God and Father of our Lord Jesus Christ, who hath blessed us with all spiritual blessings in heavenly places in Christ: According as he hath chosen us in him before the foundation of the world, that we should be holy and without blame before him in love: Having predestinated us unto the adoption of children by Jesus Christ to himself, according to the good pleasure of his will, To the praise of the glory of his grace, wherein he hath made us accepted in the beloved. In whom we have redemption through his blood, the forgiveness of sins, according to the riches of his grace; Wherein he hath abounded toward us in all wisdom and prudence; Having made known unto us the mystery of his will, according to his good pleasure which he hath purposed in himself: That in the dispensation of the fullness of times he might gather together in one all things in Christ, both which are in heaven, and which are on earth; even in him: In whom also we have obtained an inheritance, being predestinated according to the purpose of him who worketh all things after the counsel of his own will: That we should be to the praise of his glory, who first trusted in Christ."

This passage of Scripture in Ephesians tells us that God determines our life and purpose out of the pleasure of His own will. One may ask, "Why does God have the right to this supreme authority over us?" This question is borne perhaps out of the fact that we are unaware of His true identity or our unwillingness to accept the fact that He is totally in charge. Let's look at some of His attributes which more than qualify Him to be the Head and Ruler over all things.

Omnipotence: The All-Powerful God

The first attribute to consider is that He is **omnipotent**. It is a theological term that refers to the all-encompassing power of God. He is the all-powerful Lord Who has created all things and sustains them by the Word of His power. The Scripture states in Genesis 1:1-3:

> "In the beginning God created the heaven and the earth. And the earth was without form, and void; and darkness was upon the face of the deep. And the Spirit of God moved upon the face of the waters. And God said, Let there be light: and there was light."

This text proves that He is so powerful that He created and formed the world by the power of His mouth. Another text verifies this by describing Jesus' authority in Hebrews 1:3:

> "Who being the brightness of his glory, and the express image of his person, and upholding all things by the word of his power, when he had by himself purged our sins, sat down on the right hand of the Majesty on high."

His power is demonstrated and visible in the real world. This is not imaginary or perceived, but actual recognition of His unlimited, immeasurable power and authority. His power is seen in nature, history, creation and redemption. His power produces and controls and directs everything that comes to pass. Nothing in the realm of actual or conceivable things is outside of it. Amos 9:2-3 states:

> "Though they dig into hell, thence shall mine hand take them; though they climb up to heaven, thence will I bring them down: And though they hide themselves in the top of Carmel, I will search and take them out thence; and though they be hid from my sight in the bottom of the sea, thence will I command the serpent, and he shall bite them."

This ninth chapter of Amos is a continuation of Chapter 8, which deals with the justice of God passing sentence upon a provoking people. It points to the fact that no matter where the evildoer exists, God has the power to find and punish such a person for their wrongdoings. This should be a source of encouragement to every believer.

It may seem as if injustice reigns. It may seem as if evil dominates. It may seem as if wrongdoing goes unchecked and it may seem as if God's people are at the mercy of terrible oppressors. It may seem that way, but ultimately God proves Himself to be able to rule and overpower any force in heaven, on earth, and under the earth. His ability to rule and to sustain surpasses our understanding. It is very difficult for our finite (limited) minds to conceive or comprehend God's infinite (unlimited) power.

Many Scriptures attest to how powerful He is. Isaiah 55:9 declares,

"For as the heavens are higher than the earth, so are my ways higher than your ways, and my thoughts than your thoughts."

This simply means, without digging any deeper, that we cannot go up to Him to figure Him out. He has full revelation of all things; we only function in partial insight. He has come down to us through His Word and His Spirit to reveal Himself to us. The other biblical text states in Romans 11:33-36:

"O the depth of the riches both of the wisdom and knowledge of God! how unsearchable are his judgments, and his ways past finding out! For who hath known the mind of the Lord? or who hath been his counsellor? Or who hath first given to him, and it shall be recompensed unto him again? For of him, and through him, and to him, are all things: to whom be glory forever. Amen."

This passage is so powerful, describing the incomprehensibility of God's grace and goodness towards fallen humanity, specifically those whom He has chosen to be His. That is why the song "Amazing Grace" has almost become the anthem of the Christian Church.

The Reality of Redemption

One of the most powerful expressions of His omnipotence is that of redemption, which is supernatural and miraculous. It is clearly seen in the whole process of redemption of the world by our Lord Jesus Christ. Jesus being born of a woman came to save us from the penalty of sin. According to Luke 1:35-37:

"And the angel answered and said unto her, The Holy Ghost shall come upon thee, and the power of the Highest shall overshadow thee: therefore also that holy thing which shall be born of thee shall be called the Son of God. And, behold, thy cousin Elisabeth, she hath also conceived a son in her old age: and this is the sixth month with her, who was called barren. For with God nothing shall be impossible."

The working of His power in redemption is marvelously expressed through the death, burial and resurrection of Jesus Christ. This is clearly seen in Ephesians 1:19,

"And what is the exceeding greatness of his power to usward who believe, according to the working of his mighty power."

It is definitely seen in the conversion of sinners in 2 Corinthians 4:7,

"But we have this treasure in earthen vessels, that the excellency of the power may be of God, and not of us."

The Father's awesome and excellent power and workings in us is greater than our own power to do right or live right. This power is also unstoppable because it continues to spread the Good News of redemption and salvation throughout the ages. It is the seed of the Word of God that continues to be planted and multiplied in the hearts of many. It sometimes seems insignificant, but it has the power to eradicate sin and impart righteousness into the soul and mind. This passage from Matthew 13:31-32 says,

"Another parable put he forth unto them, saying, The kingdom of heaven is like to a grain of mustard seed, which a man took, and sowed in his field: Which indeed is the least of all seeds: but when it is grown, it is the greatest among herbs, and becometh a tree, so that the birds of the air come and lodge in the branches thereof."

The power of God to save is an example of how great and majestic He is. I live 40 minutes from Manhattan, New York. I seldom go into New York City because it is so busy and so congested with people. Every now and then, however, I go to see a play and have dinner with friends. I was able to see the play "Amazing Grace," which was a Broadway musical about John Newton, who wrote the hymn "Amazing Grace." This song was written in the 18th Century by an Englishman who had a slave-trading enterprise for many years. Even though he had an experience during a storm on his ship, he did not completely convert. He was convicted, but not fully changed because he continued his slave trading.

Newton's conversion became complete in 1788, 34 years after leaving his slave enterprise. Finally renouncing this profession, he wrote a letter apologizing and admitting to his offence in participating in this trade. He wrote a pamphlet entitled, "Thoughts Upon the Slave Trade," which motivated the members of Parliament to outlaw slavery in Great Britain in 1807. The song he penned reflected the immeasurable grace of God to forgive one who has committed such heinous acts against humanity.

The Paradox of Sovereignty

This power to save is beyond our understanding, but it is a true reflection of the Omnipotence of Jehovah to reach the unreachable and bring them to salvation. Is there anything that God cannot do? If He is all powerful, then He can and will do everything. This is a very sticky issue of discussion in the Church. Why? Because, there are things that we ask Him to do and they are not done. There are things that we have been waiting for and they, after many years, are not yet manifested in our lives. Is God a liar, an impostor, a player or a deceiver?

Many people (unbelievers and believers) who are discouraged and disappointed may believe that God is unfair and unjust. To the true believer, however, this is unacceptable. He does what is in keeping with His character and His purpose. There are things that God cannot do. For example, Titus 1:2 states that He cannot lie. He also cannot sin because He is holy as stated in the following passages:

> "And one cried unto another, and said, Holy, holy, holy, is the LORD of hosts: the whole earth is full of his glory" (Isaiah 6:3).

> "Because it is written, Be ye holy; for I am holy" (1 Peter 1:16).

He is a just God. His holiness will not allow Him to ignore or accept sin; therefore, He sent Christ to pay the penalty for sin, which makes it possible for our sins to be forgiven by Him. Isaiah 53:1-12 gives a striking picture of how Christ suffered so that we could be set free from the penalty of sin and escape the wrath of God.

There is another question that confronts the notion of God's omnipotence. This question is, *are all things possible with God?* Because it is possible for God to do it does not mean it is in keeping with His present and ultimate plan for the person or situation. It is not a matter of His *power* to do, but His *purpose* in doing or not doing.

To walk in agreement with Him, we must not only study, but apply His Word. In His Word, He reveals Himself to us so that we can apply His powerful, living, efficacious Word to our lives. God has a plan and a promise for each of us; spending time with Him reveals it to us. We have to trust Him that He has the power to do whatever is necessary for our lives and for His glory.

Omniscience: The All-Knowing God

We live in a world that inundates us with copious amounts of information. Knowledge about any subject is readily available on our phones, with the touch of a key on a computer keyboard, or through modern technology. In spite of the abundance of information passing to and from us minute by minute, there is no person, robot or gadget that knows everything from the beginning of time to the end of time. That privilege is totally reserved to our loving and living God and Father.

The ability to know all things throughout eternity de-scribes the **omniscience** of God. This theological term refers to God's superior knowledge and wisdom, and His power to know all things.

God is the Lord Who knows our thoughts from afar. He is acquainted with all our ways, knowing our words even before they are on our tongues. David caught a glimpse of this awe-inspiring attribute of God in Psalm 139:1-6:

> "O Lord, thou hast searched me, and known me. Thou knowest my downsitting and mine uprising, thou un-

derstandest my thought afar off. Thou compassest
my path and my lying down, and art acquainted with
all my ways. For there is not a word in my tongue,
but, lo, O Lord, thou knowest it altogether. Thou hast
beset me behind and before, and laid thine hand upon
me. Such knowledge is too wonderful for me; it is
high, I cannot attain unto it."

David continues praising God for His intimate understanding and foreknowledge:

"For thou hast possessed my reins: thou hast covered
me in my mother's womb. I will praise thee; for I am
fearfully and wonderfully made: marvellous are thy
works; and that my soul knoweth right well. My substance was not hid from thee, when I was made in
secret, and curiously wrought in the lowest parts of
the earth. Thine eyes did see my substance, yet being unperfect; and in thy book all my members were
written, which in continuance were fashioned, when
as yet there was none of them" (Ps. 139:13-16).

Isaiah also declared that the Father needs to consult no
one for knowledge or understanding:

"Who hath directed the Spirit of the Lord, or being
his counsellor hath taught him? With whom took he
counsel, and who instructed him, and taught him in
the path of judgment, and taught him knowledge,
and shewed to him the way of understanding" (Isaiah
40:13-14)?

These two passages describe the infinite wisdom and knowledge that God has, which no one else can fathom or explain. The late R.C. Sproul, in his writing on God's omniscience, declared:

> "God's omniscience comes out of His omnipotence. God is not all-knowing simply because He has applied His superior intellect to a serious study of all the universe and its contents. No, it is that God knows all because He created all and He has willed all. As the sovereign Ruler over the universe, God controls the universe. This knowledge is past finding out. God's knowledge is absolute in the sense that He is forever aware of all things. His knowledge is different from ours. We have to access to get knowledge, He is knowledge."[39]

It is so powerful and comforting to know that He knows the end from the beginning. I don't have to wonder or try to figure out what will be; I just have to consult Him, trust Him, and wait on Him.

He knew that I would be born premature. When I was born, I was so tiny that I was carried around on a pillow. I weighed just over two pounds. In 1950, in an inner-city hospital in Kingston, Jamaica, with limited equipment to care for a premature baby, there was no hope for my survival. All the doctors that my father anxiously sought refused to even touch me. They sent me home with my parents to die. My father left the hospital and ran to private doctors, hoping that they would give him some hope for me to live. They also refused to touch me. I was so weak

---

39 Sproul, R.C. *The R.C. Sproul Collection Volume 2: Essential Truths of the Christian Faith,* Carol Stream, IL: Tyndale House. 1992.

that I could not suck milk from my mother's breast. They tried to feed me with a tiny spoon, but it was very difficult to even get liquid down my throat.

My father walked away from medical science and a hopeless prognosis that said I was going to die. He came home and placed me on his bed and looked to the all-knowing God, Who brought me into this world. His prayer was, *"Lord, if You take her, I will praise You. Lord, if You let her live, I will praise You. I give her back to You."*

My stomach had been extremely distended because I was not able to take in any substance or release any substance. The moment he prayed that prayer, the omniscient God released my bowels and released my life. I have been eating since that day and definitely need to lose weight.

What is it that you feel uncertain about? Where have you been going for your answers? If you have been going to other places or to other persons, you will get limited and stilted knowledge. Go back to your prayer closet and check in with the One Who knows all things and has everything under control. Seek His face today.

> If any of you lack wisdom, let him ask of God, that giveth to all men liberally, and upbraideth not; and it shall be given him (James 1:5).

Look at the blessing we have when God is on our side. He is ever present, all-knowing and all-powerful. There is no one in the universe that can service us with these attributes. He is the only One and will always be the only One. Take time now to seek His face and wisdom for your life.

Let's continue to explore His unique attributes by next considering His **omnipresence**.

Omnipresence: The God Without Limits

The other attribute of God that is just as striking as His omnipotence and omniscience is His **omnipresence**. Omnipresence is the unlimited nature of God, and describes His ability to be in every place at all times. God is everywhere! The Bible talks about God being in every part of space. Jeremiah 23:23-24 states:

> "Am I a God at hand, saith the Lord, and not a God afar off? Can any hide himself in secret places that I shall not see him? saith the Lord. Do not I fill heaven and earth? saith the Lord."

The Lord was reminding the prophet that their words and their thoughts were not concealed from Him. Psalm 139:7-10 declares that there is nowhere in the whole universe, on land, on sea, in heaven or hell where anyone can hide from God. His presence is in all places. There isn't any place where God is not! According to the late R.C. Sproul,

> "[As] spirit, God does not occupy any place, in the sense that physical objects occupy space. The key to understanding this paradox is to think in terms of another dimension. The barrier between God and us is not a barrier of space or time."[40]

God is not only present in all places and spaces, but God is fully present in every place. That sense of His fullness should give us comfort and assurance. Believers living in New York enjoy the fullness of the presence of the God while believers in Nigeria can enjoy the same presence. His

---

40 Sproul, R.C. (1992). *Essential Truths of the Christian Faith.* Carol Streams, IL: Tyndale House Publishers.

immensity, then, does not refer to size, but His ability to be fully present everywhere. There is no place to hide from Him or escape Him.

In Good Times and Bad

There are times when we behave as if God does not see or hear. However, He never sleeps, and He never slumbers. A key verse in Proverbs 15:3 states,

> *"The eyes of the LORD are in every place, beholding the evil and the good."*

We may ask ourselves whether God saw the evil, injustice or wrong that was done to us or to someone else. But, because He never sleeps and is in all places fully at all times, then we must realize and acknowledge that He saw. Our issue, then, may be, *Why did He not act?* We must understand that wherever He is, He brings Who He is with Him. No matter what situation we are found in, He is there in justice, mercy and wisdom. His presence also assures us that He is a very present help in trouble and He is able to deliver us in the midst of what He sees.

Whether He chooses not to act in a particular moment, He yet reserves the right to be a God of justice that issues punishment and reward in His due time to "the evil and the good." This scripture destroys the myth that Christians should not face difficulties. For it is in the troubled times that His presence becomes real and necessary.

> "When thou passest through the waters, I will be with thee; and through the rivers, they shall not overflow thee: when thou walkest through the fire, thou shalt not be burned; neither shall the flame kindle upon thee" (Isaiah 43:2).

At times, we will be inundated with floods and storms; we will be burnt by fiery trials, but His presence will bring us through by His mighty hand of care and comfort. Even when He chooses not to act, He is able to minister healing and strength to our souls. When we suffer, and even endure injustice and wrong, He is able to extend to us double for our trouble:

> "For your shame ye shall have double; and for confusion they shall rejoice in their portion: therefore in their land they shall possess the double: everlasting joy shall be unto them" (Isaiah 61:7).

> "For our light affliction, which is but for a moment, worketh for us a far more exceeding and eternal weight of glory" (2 Corinthians 4:17).

The thought that God is very present at all times in every place and fully God in every place should bring great comfort to you as a reader. His presence guarantees the actual nearness of God and a real communion with Him as stated in Psalm 139:5-10. His divine omnipresence assures the believer that God is at hand to save in every place from any danger or foe and where His people need salvation. Please look back and see how many times His presence rescued, encouraged and lifted you out of difficult or even life-threatening conditions.

Just recently, in my national travel, I experienced the omnipresence and omnipotence of my God. We boarded a flight to get from one point to the other. It was an uneventful experience as we embarked on our journey. About 10 minutes after takeoff, I heard a loud noise that sounded like combustion of some sort, which shook the plane forcibly. The pilot announced that we had to return to the gate because one of the engines blew out in midair. Without question, everyone became unnerved. The pilot, after landing, came and checked us out. He was so shaken by the incident that they relieved him of his post and asked another pilot to fly another plane. I cannot imagine the possibilities of what could have happened if we were further out from our departure. It was the very present God, Who has the power to intercept and interrupt the plan and plot of every adversarial strategy and bring us safely home.

Pages would not permit me to share of how His very presence has been my comfort and consolation in all circumstances. I preached a sermon once from Psalm 46:1-3:

> "God is our refuge and strength, a very present help in trouble. Therefore will not we fear, though the earth be removed, and though the mountains be carried into the midst of the sea; Though the waters thereof roar and be troubled, though the mountains shake with the swelling thereof. Selah."

The clause that grabs me is "a very present help." The word "very" in the Hebrew is *me'od* (meh-ode') from *Strong's Concordance* OT:3966 which means "He shows up speedily and wholly." It is in the superlative, which means He shows up with "vehemence" (strength and vigor). He has revealed Himself in Ezekiel 48:35 to be Jehovah-Shammah, which means "The Lord Who is There." Indeed, there is no place where He is not. He is truly ever-present and eternal.

When I was in school in Jamaica in my childhood years, the teacher used to have roll call. She would call out each child's name and if we were there, we would raise our hand and say, "Present." This is what God says to us at any moment and in every place and time. He reaches out to us and says, "*Present!*" meaning, *I am very much here with you.*

His presence is not always felt; therefore, we cannot depend on feelings. Faith is based on knowing, not feeling. It doesn't mean that we will not sense His warmth, feel His comfort or experience His kindness. Yet, there are times when we feel nothing, see nothing and experience nothing. Life seems dark and masked with endless emptiness. It behooves every believer to hold on to God's Word and not our feelings. True belief is based on what He said. His Word can be trusted, and His promise is faithful. It is in each step of life that He shows up with His assurance and His promises.

So do not become overwhelmed by your troubling circumstances and situations. Just remember everywhere you go that you have company. Not just anyone, but the King of kings and the Lord or lords. Instead, allow the certainty of His presence to meet you at the point of your need and address the heart of your disappointment and despair. Let us rejoice in the love of a sovereign Almighty God and Father and be lavished in the comfort of His presence.

CHAPTER SIX

God in Us

BUT GODLINESS WITH CONTENTMENT IS GREAT GAIN.

1 TIMOTHY 6:6

NELSON'S BIBLE *Dictionary* gives a clear and simple meaning of godliness by stating, "Godliness means more than religious profession and a godly conduct; it also means the reality and power of a vital union with God."[41] Many definitions denote that godliness has to do with character and conduct. These two elements are based on one's love and reverence towards God. Thus, godly character is not based on one's birth, behavior, status and accomplishment.

We were born with the natural ability to oppose God and lack the ability to live for God. Why is it that we are not naturally good, godly or righteous? The Bible states it very clearly in Romans 3:23, "For all have sinned, and come short of the glory of God." Does it mean that there is not an ounce of goodness in me? My parents were preachers; I was born in a preacher's home and raised in a preacher's church. Yet, I needed to be saved, redeemed and delivered. I was born with DNA that is thoroughly corrupted by sin. My fore-parents, Adam and Eve, broke God's law and passed

41   Nelson's Illustrated Bible Dictionary, ©1986, Thomas Nelson Publishers.

down through the human lineage the inability to have God's goodness and righteousness in me. This thought can be very upsetting to the human mind.

Education=Salvation?

We were taught that there is some good in all of us and if we improve ourselves, we will be better people to others and to society. One may say that the problem with the evil that prevails in society is due to the lack of proper education. You may be an educator and have seen transformation in the lives of children who were once potentially destructive but were transformed to becoming a productive member of society. These children, perhaps, were not religious or even intend to acknowledge God, but became "good members" of their community.

This idea of education being the solution to degradation is not new. John Dewey influenced the course of the educational system in his lifetime and even to the present. Who was he? John Dewey (1859-1952) was a philosopher, educator and social reformer. He believed in the philosophy of pragmatism (rational thinking, simplicity or practicality) which gave direction on how our system of pedagogy (the method and practice of teaching) is structured. His philosophy would eventually influence how children are taught and how they would learn. He believed that when a child is trained and directed to serve and given the proper tools to guide his/herself, this child would become a credit to their community.

This is only an overview of this theory, but the gist of it is pervasive within our educational system. In other words, educate an ignorant child with proper intellectual stimulation, social skills and cultural experiences and that child will "turn out alright." Well, it depends on what you call "alright." For many, "alright" could mean finishing school, having a good job, being concerned about others, caring for one's family, maintaining a healthy life and helping to change the world. You may notice that I did not include faith-based practice in this line-up.

It is a popular thought and even a social movement that one can be "good without God." Even in the Church, we have picked up the notion that if we give our children the best education possible, they will turn out well. This means that they will not go to jail, become addicted to drugs or alcohol, practice illicit sex, commit any heinous crimes or hurt their family. We have raised a generation within the Church with these ideals. Yet parents are often shocked to know that their child became monstrous or thoroughly ungodly while they were being educated.

Do not think that I am against training, preparing and up-grading the mind. I have been through the schools of higher learning and perhaps you have been also. But the one thing those educational experiences did not have was the power to change my soul and make me "alright" with God. You see, no one can be godly without God! We were born in sin, and sin does not change because we have information. Sin only changes when we accept the Sacrifice of the Blood that Jesus shed on the Cross over 2,000 years ago.

The Bible states in Romans 3:23, "For all have sinned, and come short of the glory of God." This sinful tendency has nothing to do with the ability to do Math, Science, English, or any other subject. It has to do with the inability to please God while living in an evil world. We will come short of the glory of God with or without a proper education. What does it mean "to come short of the glory of God?"

Well first, let us consider the primary question, *"What is sin?" Strong's Dictionary* defines sin as NT:264 *hamartano* (ham-ar-tan'-o); "to miss the mark." Let us look at the game of darts, which may be a clearer way to explain missing the mark. The game requires a dart board with a center ring and several outer rings. The goal of this game is to throw a sharp, pointed implement and aim for the center ring. If it goes right into the center, then the person wins the game.

The righteousness of God is the center ring, the dart is our life and the throwing of the dart is the way we try to live a godly life. Everyone who is born tries to throw their dart and hit the center ring of God's goodness, holiness and righteousness. However, no one on earth, since the fall of Adam and Eve, has ever been and will ever have the ability to throw the dart of their life and hit the center of His righteousness. The only way to strike out sin is to surrender our lives to the Lord Jesus Christ Who gave His life so that we can put God in the center of it all.

The Fallacy of Morality

Another fallacy concerning what it takes to live a "good life" is the notion of morality. Likened to a good education, the purpose of morality is to assist the person in becoming a better member of society. The educated, morally good person is the ideal person to help make the world a better place through the sheer force of their righteous and acceptable behavior. What does it mean to be morally good? We need to know, because if we become decent, honest and ethical people, then the crime rate would go down and some of the other ills of society could be eliminated.

What is morality? A definition taken from a website entitled "All About Philosophy" describes morality as such:

"Morality speaks of a system of behavior with regards
to standards of right or wrong behavior. The word
carries the concepts of: (1) moral standards, with
regard to behavior; (2) moral responsibility, refer-
ring to our conscience; and (3) a moral identity, or
one who is capable of right or wrong action. Common synonyms include ethics, principles, virtue, and
goodness."[42]

This definition gives us the gist of what we expect from a
person who believes that he/she is living a clean life.

The Bible asks the question in Job 14:4, "Who can bring a
clean thing out of an unclean? not one." *Barnes Commentary*
explains this question in a way that I hope you understand
the human inability to be truly godly, even in our attempt to
be truly moral. Barnes states:

"This is evidently a proverb or an adage... Probably,
however, it is designed as a plea of mitigation for his
conscious frailties and infirmities. He could not but
admit that he had faults. But he asks, how could it be
expected to be otherwise? He belonged to a race that
was sinful and depraved...This passage is of great value as showing the early opinion of the world in regard to the native character of man. The sentiment
was undoubtedly common – so common as to have
passed into a proverb – that man was a sinner; and
that it could not be expected that anyone of the race
should be pure and holy."

He goes on to say:

"The nature of the lion, the tiger, the hyaena, the ser-

---

42   https://www.allaboutphilosophy.org/morality.htm.

pent is propagated, and so the same thing is true of man. It is a great law, that the offspring will resemble the parentage; and as the offspring of the lion is not a lamb but a young lion; or a wolf is not a kid but a young wolf, so the offspring of man is not an angel, but is a man with the same nature, the same moral character, the same proneness to evil with the parent...As a historical record, this passage proves that the doctrine of original sin was early held in the world. Still it is true that the same great law prevails, that the offspring of woman is a sinner-no matter where he may be born, or in what circumstances he may be placed. No art, no philosophy, no system of religion can prevent the operation of this great law under which we live, and by which we die...."[43]

It is very clear that the human race was thoroughly corrupted with Adam and Eve's fall from God's will and presence due to their sin. This sinful nature was passed on through our lineage and became lodged in our DNA, which rendered us incapable of being holy, righteous or good. Therefore, nothing we do can become good. The action or behavior may appear to be good, but the motive and life behind it are still corrupted.

I was raised in Christian home. My father and mother were preachers, teachers and pastors. There was never, ever a day that I can remember that Christian principles and activities were not expressed within my home. There were always morning, evening and mealtime prayers; there was always Bible reading and discussion, and there was always church attendance and participation. This continued

43 Barnes' Notes, Electronic Database. © 1997 by Biblesoft.

all the way to their dying day. Yet, when I was born, I did not become a believer because of my environment or due to my lineage. I had to at some point receive Jesus as my personal Savior. In the midst of it all, I was born a sinner baby. This means I had to reckon with my inability to be genuinely good, and continually righteous. I had to own at the age of 13 that Christ was the answer to my sinfulness. I, then, received Jesus as my Lord, which gave me the power to live a godly life. This doesn't just apply to me, but to everyone and anyone who wants to be holy and righteous. Doing good works and performing kind deeds will not make us godly people. Ephesians 2:8-9 stresses this:

> "For by grace are ye saved through faith; and that not of yourselves: it is the gift of God; Not of works, lest any man should boast."

The word "works" in this passage makes it very clear that we cannot live out the nature of God without Him. *Strong's Dictionary* defines "works" as NT:2041 *ergon* (er'-gon); "from a primary (but obsolete) *ergo* (to work); toil (as an effort or occupation); by implication, an act: KJV–deed, doing, labour, work."[44]

My salvation, my desire to be godly, and my ability to do good deeds are not dependent on my accomplishments or achievements. I am totally dependent on the Lord's power in my life to be godly. Does this mean that Christians should not strive to be moral or ethical in their lifestyle? We are born with a conscience because we were created in the image of God. Sin, however, caused us to lose the likeness of God to be holy and righteous. Although we do

---

44 Biblesoft's New Exhaustive Strong's Numbers and Concordance with Expanded Greek-Hebrew Dictionary. © 1994, Biblesoft and International Bible Translators, Inc.

still know right from wrong, within we lack the power to do righteously. Adam and Eve had the instruction from Almighty God and they still disobeyed, thus causing every human being to want to disobey. The Israelites had the Ten Commandments but continually broke those laws. There was never a time in history that people were unaware of what was right and wrong. Moral, ethical behavior was always demanded so that society would be a safe and peaceful place to live. The issue, then, is not mere morality, but where we get our dictates for being godly and right in our heart, mind and work.

To Have Eternal Life

I am reminded of the account in Scripture of the rich young ruler. This wealthy young man ran to Jesus, seeking an audience with Him. He knew about inheritance, because being young and rich, he had to have gotten his portion from his father. He now inquires of the Master Teacher, Jesus, how he can have life beyond the earthly life. He had everything else but wanted to set himself up for his eternity. He asks Jesus in Matthew 19:16,

> "Good Master, what good thing shall I do, that I may have eternal life?"

He wanted to do good things. In other words, he wanted to be a morally responsible member of the community. Jesus proceeded to challenge him in Verse 17 about the code of moral conduct, which was the Ten Commandments.

> "And he said unto him, Why callest thou me good? there is none good but one, that is, God: but if thou wilt enter into life, keep the commandments."

After inquiring about which commandments, the young man responded in confidence in Matthew 19:20:

> "The young man saith unto him, All these things have I kept from my youth up: what lack I yet?"

His response revealed that he was very sure that he was "good," because in his eyes he obeyed all the commandments, which proved that he qualified to have eternal life without difficulty. The young ruler then asked if he lacked anything else. Jesus gave him the answer in Matthew 19:21:

> "Jesus said unto him, If thou wilt be perfect, go and sell that thou hast, and give to the poor, and thou shalt have treasure in heaven: and come and follow me."

It is obvious that this young man was morally and ethically good in his own eyes. He followed the moral code of his Jewish religion and apparently was an outstanding member of his community. What then was lacking in the eyes of Jesus? Although Mark's account of this incident confirmed that Jesus "beholding him loved him" (Mark 10:21), our Lord challenged the young man's so-called "goodness" and pointed to a higher way of living, which is to be "perfect." This word, according to *Strong's* dictionary, is "NT:5046, *teleios* (tel'-i-os); from NT:5056; 'complete' (in various applications of labor, growth, mental and moral character, etc.); (as noun, with NT:3588) completeness: KJV–of full age, man, perfect."[45]

In other words, there is a godly way to live and that life must be dictated by what Jesus says. Godliness is not

---

45   Biblesoft's New Exhaustive Strong's Numbers and Concordance with Expanded Greek-Hebrew Dictionary. © 1994, Biblesoft and International Bible Translators, Inc.

just complying with rules and regulations but obeying the teachings and principles which Jesus defines in the Bible. It does not mean that we should not do what the commandments demand, but it does mean that we cannot practice them as rituals, if we wish to live a life that is pleasing to God. The bottom line is that my godliness and every believer's godliness are directly connected to our relationship with the Lord Jesus Christ. I can do all the good in the world, and I should do good, but if I do not have the Spirit of Christ in my life, then I will be lacking in the same way the rich young ruler went away lacking. He was ultimately asked to sell all his goods and give them to the poor and he could not bring himself to do that. It was easy for him to brag about the rules he kept, but he failed to follow the command of the Master Teacher, Who came down from the righteous and wise God.

Embracing Godliness

How can I then become godly in my daily life? How can I strive to be godly? It doesn't come naturally! Nor does it come behaviorally! It doesn't come by being intellectual! To walk and live in godliness, one must embrace more than religious profession and godly conduct; it also means "the reality and power of a vital union with God."[46] It encompasses the gamut of Christian living. Paul further illustrates this definition by declaring in 1 Timothy 4:8,

> "For bodily exercise profiteth little: but godliness is profitable unto all things, having promise of the life that now is, and of that which is to come."

---

46   Nelson's Illustrated Bible Dictionary, ©1986, Thomas Nelson Publishers.

It is also supported by 2 Peter 1:6-8:

> "And to knowledge temperance; and to temperance patience; and to patience godliness; And to godliness brotherly kindness; and to brotherly kindness charity. For if these things be in you, and abound, they make you that ye shall neither be barren nor unfruitful in the knowledge of our Lord Jesus Christ."

Scholars connote that godliness includes knowledge, reverence, affection, submission and obedience to God. McClintock and Strong's Bible Dictionary breaks down a paradigm for godliness that we can follow which is:

> "knowledge in the mind, by which it is distinguished from the visions of the superstitious; rectitude in the conscience, that distinguishes it from hypocrisy; sacrifice in the life, or renunciation of the world, by which it is distinguished from the unmeaning obedience of him who goes as a happy constitutions leads him; and, lastly, zeal in the heart, which differs from the languishing emotions of the lukewarm."[47]

Let us use this listing to design a framework which we can use to cultivate godliness.

The first one is "knowledge in the mind." This is not secular knowledge of science, history, literature and the like. This is divine knowledge for righteous living. *Unger's Dictionary* talks about this knowledge and how we can acquire it. The expression "to know" sometimes means "to approve of and take delight in where God reveals Himself," which is in the Word of God.

---

47   McClintock and Strong Encyclopedia, Electronic Database. © 2000, Biblesoft.

"Blessed is the man that walketh not in the counsel of the ungodly, nor standeth in the way of sinners, nor sitteth in the seat of the scornful. But his delight is in the law of the Lord; and in his law doth he meditate day and night. And he shall be like a tree planted by the rivers of water, that bringeth forth his fruit in his season; his leaf also shall not wither; and whatsoever he doeth shall prosper" (Psalm 1:1-3).

This psalm suggests that if we meditate, think on, mutter, and rehearse God's Word daily, it will make us healthy and whole in our minds and lives. This is how we get to know God and discover what He desires for our lives, which is the path of godliness. Another way to know is to understand that God is working things out in every circumstance in our lives. This assurance of care and protection is borne out of our understanding of the character of God. If I believe that He is good and true, then it will influence how I perceive my problems and difficulties. This is why Paul declared in Romans 8:28:

"And we know that all things work together for good to them that love God, to them who are the called according to his purpose."

Paul did not say here that He feels as if things will work out. He did not say he hoped that things would be better. He emphatically stated that He "knows" that God, based on His power and character, was working it all for Paul's good. This is the knowledge that will keep us from panicking or performing differently from what God wants for us.

Remember! We can only obey God when we respond to His godliness.

Loving the Lord

The next aspect of knowing God is loving Him. The Bible states in 1 Corinthians 8:3, "But if any man love God, the same is known of him." The person who loves God or who is committed to Him is acknowledged and approved by God and accepted as His own. What a wonderful privilege and a precious opportunity! To love Him, we must first be known by Him. It is the will of God that we know Him, but first we must recognize that He knows us. When we receive Him in our hearts, we will love Him and serve Him. John 17:3 declares this, "And this is life eternal, that they might know thee the only true God, and Jesus Christ, whom thou hast sent." The Apostle John in 1 John 2:3-5 sums it up clearly:

> "And hereby we do know that we know him, if we keep his commandments. He that saith, I know him, and keepeth not his commandments, is a liar, and the truth is not in him. But whoso keepeth his word, in him verily is the love of God perfected: hereby know we that we are in him."

In other words, to know Him and to be known by Him will cause us to love and obey Him. This relationship produces godliness. We are often checked by our consciences. Having a God-conscious awareness of what is godly and ungodly is a great asset to the believer's life. What is a godly conscience? It is "a person's inner awareness of conforming to the will of God or departing from it, resulting in either a sense of approval or condemnation."[48] The believer's conscience, however, has been cleansed by the Blood of Jesus Christ.

---

48 Nelson's Illustrated Bible Dictionary, ©1986, Thomas Nelson Publishers.

"How much more shall the blood of Christ, who through the eternal Spirit offered himself without spot to God, purge your conscience from dead works to serve the living God?" (Hebrews 9:14).

This consciousness of His will comes from being continually influenced by the Word and will of God. We have to pray and ask God to make our consciences sensitive to His Word and also sensitive to anything that displeases Him. Naturally the spirit of the age and this present world are purposed to dull our spiritual senses to the Spirit and Word of God. We must continually yield our lives to the Lord, and seek to make our hearts tender to the Lord. David cried out for his mind, heart and spirit to become cleansed and purified in Psalm 51. He desired to have a mind that was sensitive to the will of God, after he had followed his heart and will in his affair with Bathsheba.

Not Our Will, But His

The greatest demand on the believer's life from the Lord is obedience. Obedience is doing what someone else wants or desires. Throughout the Bible, obedience was used as the measuring stick of one's love and devotion to God. I often say that we can check and determine the quality of our spirituality by how obedient we are willing to be to the Word of God. I am as spiritual as I am obedient. Without obedience, one's spirituality and "godliness" is just an act.

"Having a form of godliness, but denying the power thereof: from such turn away" (2 Timothy 3:5).

Abraham, Moses, Esther, Ruth, Jeremiah, Mary, Joseph, Paul, John, just to name a few, followed God and fulfilled

God's purpose in their lives. Jesus was, of course, the Ultimate Example of obedience to God the Father. Christ "humbled himself, becoming obedient even unto death, yea, the death of the cross" (Phil. 2:8). Because we are believers in Christ and have taken on His life into our life, Peter calls us "children of obedience" (1 Peter 1:14). Being an obedient child simply means that our behavior demonstrates agreement and fulfillment of God's command, along with submission to His will and trusting His Word and way for our lives. We need to rehearse Proverbs 3:5-6 continually:

> "Trust in the Lord with all thine heart; and lean not unto thine own understanding. In all thy ways acknowledge him, and he shall direct thy paths."

The acknowledgment here means to recognize that He is Lord and that He deserves to be in charge. If we follow Him, we will have godly guidance, knowledge and results. We can live godly! This cannot be done by just behaving right, because there is no ability to do right without the only right One, Jesus, living in our lives. If we want to live righteously, we must get to know Him, love Him, trust Him and obey Him. May this be your daily desire, as I pray that it will always be mine!

CHAPTER SEVEN
The Progressive Walk

THERE ARE times when we all feel as if we are not making progress in our walk with the Lord. Many people stray from the Christian Faith because they fell short in some area of their journey. Yes, even the best of saints can make poor choices and leave the Faith. Weaknesses, failures, challenges, disappointments and discouragements are just a few of the reasons why we may want to give up on the notion of living a godly life.

Many churches teach that when someone accepts the Lord Jesus as their personal Savior, that person will no longer have personal struggles, desires or feelings towards anything ungodly. This teaching is based on the notion that this new convert is fully sanctified, set apart and free from any ungodly appetite. When, however, the believer experiences temptation and longings or even gives in to these desires, it can be devastating. It is vital that new believers learn that sinful yearnings do not disappear at salvation.

What is the believer then to do? Should they give up and go back into the world? Should they live a double life — one way in the Church and another in the world? Many are discouraged by this challenging new walk. This chapter, therefore, is designed to encourage and instruct you how to live for God, if you follow His Word and trust His way.

The Sanctification Journey

The only way to continue in the path of godliness is to know the Scriptures. Get to know the Word and it will help to increase your faith in Jesus Christ, which in turn will strengthen your walk daily. This process of daily walking with the Lord is called **sanctification**. It is sometimes noted as being set apart, separated or chosen to live for God. It is defined as:

> "The process of God's grace by which the believer is separated from sin and becomes dedicated to God's righteousness. Accomplished by the Word of God (John 17:17) and the Holy Spirit (Romams 8:3-4), sanctification results in holiness, or purification from the guilt and power of sin."[49]

Let us look at these passages. The dictionary says we are sanctified, separated by the Word of God from sin. The Lord Jesus prayed in His high priestly prayer in John 17:17:

> "Sanctify them through thy truth: thy word is truth."

This means that when we read the Word and apply its truths within our daily lives, we will become more influenced by Christ than we are attracted to the world. This is an ongoing experience that requires daily reading, daily studying, daily rehearsing and daily practicing. Reader, I am sure that you can remember a Word from the Scriptures that grabbed you or stuck with you to the point where you could not get it out of your mind. The more you thought about it and embraced it, the more it became part of your thinking, which affected your behavior. That is how the Word sanctifies us, cleanses us and transforms us.

49   Nelson's Illustrated Bible Dictionary, © 1986, Thomas Nelson Publishers.

The next agent in our sanctification process is the Person of the Holy Spirit. Our previously mentioned definition of sanctification referenced Romans 8:3-6:

> "For what the law could not do, in that it was weak through the flesh, God sending his own Son in the likeness of sinful flesh, and for sin, condemned sin in the flesh: That the righteousness of the law might be fulfilled in us, who walk not after the flesh, but after the Spirit. For they that are after the flesh do mind the things of the flesh; but they that are after the Spirit the things of the Spirit. For to be carnally minded is death; but to be spiritually minded is life and peace."

This is a powerful text which gives us the understanding of the dynamics between our spirit and the Holy Spirit's activity in our walk with the Lord. The gist of the passage has to do with our walk. The word "walk" in the text comes from the Greek word *peripateo* (per-ee-pat-eh'-o) which means our "deportment, lifestyle and activities." According to the passage, we can choose to live by walking after our fleshly, carnal ways or by following the leading of the Holy Spirit. The fleshy carnal ways are the sinful, selfish and godless thoughts and deeds that we committed freely before we got saved. Those thoughts and deeds do not die out of our lives when we get saved, but they can be kept in check and under the power of God when we obey the Holy Spirit's leading.

What will the Holy Spirit say to us to keep us in check? He will speak what is revealed and only what is revealed in the Bible. The Holy Spirit will speak to us through a song that has biblical principles, or through a sermon. He will speak a Word to our minds, or He will send someone to give us counsel. All of these methods of conveying the message will be in keeping with what God says in His Word. You may get an important message by text, email, regular mail, phone call, Federal Express or in person. The bottom line is that you will receive the message the best way you can hear. Sometimes we have to hear it over and over again in order for us to receive it. The Holy Spirit's job is to make sure you receive whatever is necessary to become what God desires of you.

When the Lord spoke to me about leaving nursing and going into full time ministry, I was very upset and became confused. I could not see myself leaving a good paying nursing job as a nurse practitioner to go into full-time service, not knowing how I would take care of myself. It was a very difficult choice, but He confirmed it with His Word. This is the passage He gave me and the passage I now live by in Matthew 6:33-34:

> "But seek ye first the kingdom of God, and his righteousness; and all these things shall be added unto you. Take therefore no thought for the morrow: for the morrow shall take thought for the things of itself. Sufficient unto the day is the evil thereof."

This was my guiding light, along with key persons in my life affirming it with good counsel. It was not an easy decision, but at this point in my life it has been a God-given blessing that I will never regret.

You may be at a crossroads in your life, but remember you are called to be separated from the world. So obey His Word and follow His Spirit and you will experience the peace of the Lord.

Producing Holiness

The other portion of the definition mentioned earlier talks about the result of being set apart or sanctified. The purpose of this spiritual walk is to produce holiness in our lives. Why holiness? God is holy. We therefore strive to become more and more like Him.

> "But as he which hath called you is holy, so be ye holy in all manner of conversation; Because it is written, Be ye holy; for I am holy" (1 Peter 1:15-16).

We will never be perfectly holy as He is, but as we walk daily in Him and closely to Him, we become more and more like Him.

What is holiness? Most Bible dictionaries note that holiness means "to be sanctified, godly or set apart to serve and please God." *The Westminster Catechism*'s first question is: "What is the chief end of man?" The catechism states: "Man's chief end is to glorify God and to enjoy Him forever." This is the crux of sanctification, which is to give over our lives to God and to enjoy His benefits for our lives.

Crucified With Christ

Please join me in examining this verse of scripture from Galatians 2:20, which will guide us to better understand how to continue walking in godliness and embracing the sanctification process in our daily lives:

> "I am crucified with Christ: nevertheless I live; yet not I, but Christ liveth in me: and the life which I now live in the flesh I live by the faith of the Son of God, who loved me, and gave himself for me" (Gal. 2:20).

The passage states that we who are believers have been crucified with Christ. This means that when Jesus went to the Cross and died, our sins were also nailed to that Cross. It happened once and for all. The sin here is our sin nature, meaning what we inherited from Adam and Eve. It means we are no longer bound to sin or have to give in to sin.

Accepting what Jesus did means we are forgiven and now have the power to resist and say no to any sinful act. When we were not saved, we did not have this power or desire to stop sinning. It is not in our nature to want to stop sinning against God. But, when we hand over our called souls to God, His crucifixion nails our love and weakness for sin to the Cross. When He arose, we also came up with a new desire and power to walk away from sin. If we do sin, it is because we want to and not because we must.

Hold on to this, believer, because it is your lifeline to victory! Let's say you are hanging out with friends from your past and they are asking you to do what you used to do before you were saved. They do not understand your conversion and they assume that your lifestyle is the same. The things that they are asking you to do are very familiar to you and they may have given you some pleasure.

You could go along with it, but you have another Spirit working in you dictating to you the choice you should make. You are not in this moment by yourself. The Holy Spirit is there guiding and empowering you to please God instead of yourself and your friends. If you follow God, it is because you have the power to do so. If you follow your friends, it is because you choose to do so. There is never a time that a true believer can say that they couldn't help themselves or that "the devil made them do it." I hope you understand what it means to be crucified with Christ!

This is what the Bible says about our state and status in Him in Romans 6:9-14:

> "Knowing that Christ being raised from the dead dieth no more; death hath no more dominion over him. For in that he died, he died unto sin once: but in that he liveth, he liveth unto God. Likewise ***reckon ye also yourselves to be dead indeed unto sin, but alive unto God through Jesus Christ our Lord***. Let not sin therefore reign in your mortal body, that ye should obey it in the lusts thereof. Neither yield ye your members as instruments of unrighteousness unto sin: but yield yourselves unto God, as those that are alive from the dead, and your members as instruments of righteousness unto God. For sin shall not have dominion over you: for ye are not under the law, but under grace."

The key point is that whoever or whatever you listen to and yield to is what you will perform. If you listen to God, you will live and act for Him, but if you listen to yourself, the devil, the world or others, you will yield to them. You have the glorious power of choice to walk in a godly way and have peace with God.

In the second clause of Galatians 2:20, I want you to see the result of our sin being nailed to the Cross:

> *"Nevertheless I live; yet not I, but Christ liveth in me..."*

Death to the old way is accomplished, but at the same time, we live. We now have life in Christ. This means we are now living with a different kind of life in us. The old life is overpowered by the new life. It is not our life that desires holiness, godliness or righteousness, but the new life is operating and producing right choices.

Where did this new life come from? It kicked in when we received Jesus as our personal Lord and Savior. One of the key words in the clause is "liveth." This means this life continues, meaning it operates in us daily.

How does it operate? It operates through the Word of God and the guidance of the Holy Spirit. You see, this life is strange to us. We are used to living according to what we feel, see and desire. All those things, even the innocent ones, are not pleasing to God. This new life in Christ is designed to teach us how to live to please Him and not ourselves or others. To continue the walk of godliness, we have to take heed to the life of Christ in us by going to Bible study, having daily devotions, seeking godly counsel in decisions, and making hard choices in favor of God. It also means we must worship, which entails singing, praying, meditating and speaking His Word. It also means we must spend time with people who are doing the same thing.

It doesn't mean you avoid unbelievers, but it means that you will be strengthened when you fellowship with godly people. A baby cannot grow if it is not fed throughout the day and night. That principle goes for the soul. A soul that houses the life of Christ must be fed continuously with His Word and His will. According to 1 Peter 2:2, "As newborn babes, desire the sincere milk of the word, that ye may grow thereby." Desire His Word and feed on it so that the life of Christ will overpower the will of the flesh and the devil!

Finally, the last clause of Galatians 2:20 notes:

> *"...I live by the faith of the Son of God, who loved me, and gave himself for me."*

This clause tells us how we can live this new, godly life of Christ daily. It is by faith in Jesus that we receive forgiveness from our sins. We must also trust and believe that His blood was powerful enough to eradicate our sins, and that we have been accepted by the Father into the family of God. It means that faith is the key to our walk. If we truly believe it, we will act upon it. This faith is based on our knowledge of how much Jesus loved us and gave Himself for us. This love is beyond our comprehension. It is so strong and powerful that it pulls us to love and to obey Him. This is the reason the enemy wants us to be ignorant of His love. When we do not read or study the Bible, we will be clueless concerning Jesus' love and care for us. When we recognize how deep, pure and lasting His love is toward us, we will believe more and more in Him and His life will grow stronger and stronger in us.

The Apostle Paul recognized how privileged he was to have Jesus' life in his life and what a great transformation was wrought in him. He declared in 2 Corinthians 5:17, "Therefore if any man be in Christ, he is a new creature: old things are passed away; behold, all things are become new." This is every believer's testimony. We are a new creation because we are now into Christ and not into ourselves. Old ways are not dominating our thoughts and lifestyle because we are becoming new in Him every day through His Word and His presence.

Sanctified From Sin

How can a believer claim to live godly and still fall into sin every now and then? Remember that we are still in the flesh. This flesh is still prone to temptation. Temptation is not a sin, but only when we yield to it. Yielding causes us to fall and to commit sin against God and compromise our walk and blow our testimony. Should we give up and feel hopeless? No!!! God loves us so deeply that He knows that we are prone to fall. This new walk with Christ is so strange and different that it is all a learning process.

Let's go back to school. Or, better yet, let's go back to my school. In high school, I was a good student, but the one subject that stumped me was geometry. I did well in the sciences and all other math courses, but geometry created a mental block in my mind. I had to get a tutor, but even then, it took a while for me to finally get it. Although I failed geometry the first quarter, I stayed with it until I passed it at the end of the semester.

Is that happening to you in some area of your life right now? Perhaps you are an angry person and cannot seem to shake the spirit of anger. You may say mean things; do mean things and think mean things. You want to be nice, but it just doesn't come up when you interact with others. The Lord, however, is constantly pulling you to change your heart and mind through His Word and His love. Do not give up! Just as I did not give up on geometry and finally passed it, you will come through and release the angry spirit and experience the joy and peace of the Lord.

Whatever the sin or struggle, God has the answer. Where is the answer? Of course it is found in the Bible. The Bible has the answer to every need in our soul. The verse that will help us with the question of the believer's sins and failures after salvation is found in 1 John 1:9-10:

> "If we confess our sins, he is faithful and just to forgive us our sins, and to cleanse us from all unrighteousness. If we say that we have not sinned, we make him a liar, and his word is not in us."

Let us examine Verse 10! It suggests that we should be honest about our sins and failures. You see, if we do not accept the fact that we have tendencies and weaknesses that are not godly, we will become a hypocrite and live a double life in the Church. Or, we will stay away from church because we have given up on ourselves. Jesus has made a way for us to live honestly and grow in Him. We do not have to hide or pretend. We may not be able tell the whole world our worst secret, but we can tell it to Jesus. He will help us, even in our weakest moments.

This is what He says about our weak, feeble and frail flesh: "My grace is sufficient for thee: for my strength is made perfect in weakness" (2 Corinthians 12:9). God promised to help Paul in his infirmities and afflictions. We can apply this same Word because we also need help in our moments of failures.

The Necessity to Confess

Verse Nine of John's first epistle is the key to our quest. If we sin or fall, we are encouraged in this verse to "confess" it. Meaning, we must "tell it" or "own it". Did Jesus see us when we sinned? Yes! But we must own it, because if we do not acknowledge our wrongdoing, we are saying that we did not really do anything wrong. If we believe that it was not wrong, we will continue to do it, which means we will continue to sin. The word "confess" in this verse is the Greek word *homologeo* (hom-ol-og-eh'-o), which means "to acknowledge and to agree." It is to say the same thing God is saying about the sin. Agreement is necessary so that change will occur.

I can say that stealing is wrong, but still believe that there are times that it is permissible to steal. The word "if" in the verse suggests that there may be times that I may not agree. Why would I not confess my sin to God? I may think that it's not all that bad. I may also think that because of the way I was raised, I cannot change. I may say that everybody else is doing it and they are blessed. So many excuses can be given to avoid the confession or agreement that this thought or deed offends God. The confession or failure to confess is not dependent on how I feel, popular opinion, culture or church. It is dependent on what God says in His Word.

For example, gossip doesn't seem as heinous as rape or terrorism. Yet, it can be just as damaging to the human life as the deeds of a rapist or terrorist. Spreading lies, defaming character and revealing failures can destroy someone for the rest of their lives. Church can be fertile ground for gossip, because many believers do not see it as "bad" as other crimes. If a believer feels that it is not terrible, then that believer will not feel the need to confess. If there is no confession or agreement that this is a sin, the gossip will continue and that person's walk will be ungodly and cause others to walk in ungodliness.

The Bible states in Proverbs 18:8: "The words of a talebearer are as wounds, and they go down into the innermost parts of the belly." The word for "talebearer" is the Hebrew word *nirgan* (neer-gawn'), which means "slanderer or whisperer." This is someone who tears people's character down with their mouth. This person wounds and destroys hearts and lives with words. The talebearer must see that it is offensive to God and destructive to others. It requires confession and brokenness before God.

David declares in Psalm 51:17, "The sacrifices of God are a broken spirit: a broken and a contrite heart, O God, thou wilt not despise." It literally means that when I come to God crushed and downcast, in this case due to my sin, He will not scorn me or turn me away. He will help me. He will assist me in the process of my change.

How, then, will Jesus help me when I truly confess and agree that I am wrong and want to get it right so that I can live a godly life? The ninth verse from First John Chapter One says that Jesus is "faithful" (trustworthy) and "just" (righteous) to "forgive" me (to release me of the penalty of my sin). This is a wonderful promise that Jesus makes to every sincere believer who humbly submits their sins, faults and failures to the Lord. He will always forgive us when we choose to agree that what we have done is wrong and we want to get it right.

The Process of Purging

The latter clause of 1 John 1:9 has to do with what happens after the forgiveness. The work of the Holy Spirit will now take this forgiven soul and take it through spiritual rehabilitation. You see sin leaves a stain, and it will take the sanctification process to lift the stain and residue of sin out of our souls.

The clause says: "...and to cleanse us from all unrighteousness." The Spirit of Christ will cleanse us from the sin that we have been forgiven from. What does the word "cleanse" mean here? The Greek word for cleanse is *katharizo* (kath-ar-id'-zo) which means to purge or to purify. It is the root word of "catharsis," an experience in which things are brought to the surface. Purging and purifying is time consuming, which means one goes through a process.

I remember as a little girl my mother took me to the country for summer vacation in the parish of Clarendon in

Jamaica, West Indies. My great uncle owned a great house with much land surrounding it. I was extremely taken aback with the beauty of the landscaping, the freshness of the country air and the healthy tastefully prepared food from the farm and from the stall.

One of the greatest joys of the trip that fascinated me the most was going down by the river. You see, the river ran right through my great uncle's property, and it was where all the women met to do laundry. To a young girl of about nine years old who was raised in the city, seeing the women wash clothes in the river was terribly different and captivating. I observed that the white towels and sheets were lily white and spotless.

I decided to sit by the river and experience the washing of clothes by the river. I watched how they placed lime and special natural ingredients on strong stains, placed the linens in the sun for a while, scrubbed them and then washed and rinsed them in the river. Perhaps it is hard for us to understand how those clothing articles became so white without today's detergents and bleaches; but it was the manual washing, scrubbing and natural bleaching that removed the stains.

This is what comes to mind when I think of how God sanctifies my soul with that same diligent purging and cleansing. He applies His Word to my heart and mind through the operation of the Holy Spirit, which in turn convicts and convinces me of sin or offense. This conviction causes me to repent —that is, to change my mind about the matter — and then takes me on a journey of re-education. This re-education through the Word, teaches me how to do it God's way. It might take learning this over and over again, until it becomes easy and joyful to do.

Let me take you to a point in my life when I had to forgive someone very dear to me. You see, the sanctification process deals with every matter of the heart and soul. I was always a good student in school. I enjoyed learning and strove to excel academically as much as I could. There were times throughout my grade and middle school period that I received special certificates, recognition and accolades. My mother was always present, but my father was always absent.

At every graduation, I looked in the audience and he was never there. I held him hostage in my heart concerning his absence at these crucial times in my life when I needed his support. I prayed and asked the Lord to help me to deal with the negative emotions that crept into my spirit whenever I thought about my father in this matter.

One day, the Lord sent help and delivered me from the anger I had towards my father. My father called me into his bedroom and gave me a check to cover my tuition for grad school. I was truly amazed, because he had never supported my education financially up to this point. He had tears in his eyes and made this confession. He said that he was so sorry that he never attended any of my school functions. He went on to say that he too had ambitions to further his education, particularly to attend seminary. When he tried to pursue it, he was rejected because of the color of his skin. The only seminary opportunity that opened up was the Adventist seminary, which he passed up.

Therefore, when he saw me advancing my educational goals, he became envious. He then asked me to forgive him. We both were washed with tears. We hugged each other and felt the cleansing and healing power of God. I immediately forgave him and forgot the so-called offense. I also asked him to forgive me for resenting him and not thinking about his struggles.

This is what the sanctification process is designed to do for us and through us, if we will yield to the Holy Spirit. Do not give up on yourself in your progressive journey because of failures and downfalls. Trust the Lord Who saved you to continue to transform you.

CHAPTER EIGHT

The Enemies of Contentment

L IFE IN this present world can bring joy, sadness and difficulty into our lives. Even if we moved to Mars, as some people are planning and hoping to do, we would find enemies up there as well. The Lord Jesus warned His disciples that in this world they would be hated (Mark 13:13). The word "hated" in this text means to be "persecuted," to be "detested" and sometimes it means "to loved less." This means that there are times when we will be mocked, rejected, ostracized and even punished for our belief in Christ Jesus as Savior and Lord.

It is very difficult for the average Christian in the Western world to imagine what it is like to be severely punished, imprisoned, mutilated or killed because they go church, read the Bible or speak the Name of Jesus publicly. Yet, it happens every day in other countries. Christians in these countries live with the reality of being martyred for their faith daily. There is a Christian magazine entitled "The Voice of the Martyrs." They report on the activities of Christian persons, ministries and churches all over the world. They specialize in exposing the persecutions that individuals and churches experience so that the Church at large can pray for and support these brave believers. In a recent excerpt from that magazine:

"Church leaders and students were recently arrested and over 50 churches closed. The Wa region is
one of the most secretive places on earth. Christians
in the Wa Special Region of Myanmar have long endured persecution, but the situation has worsened,
according to the BBC. Bordering China in East Shan
State, it is under the Myanmar Government, yet Chi-
nese Communists still control the laws and limit the
use of phones and electricity. In the last few months,
the crackdown on practicing Christianity has been
widely felt throughout the area. Ninety-two pastors
have been arrested with no indication of their release; three church buildings have been burnt and
destroyed, while 52 churches have been closed. The
HuTuawng Lasho Bible School has been closed and
41 of its students, arrested."[50]

Many people leave churches because they were offended
by an usher, a pew member, a pastor or the message. These
persecuted believers who are being killed for the faith have
no such luxury or choice to run from one cushioned church
pew to another because of some minor offence. They are
constantly declaring their commitment and allegiance to
Christ with their lives. We cannot even imagine this kind
of suffering for the Faith. Yet, we have to admit the persecution is now showing its ugly head in America.

In the November 2017 *Christianity Today* article, "Are
American churches under attack?", Harry Farley states
that since 1980, there have been more than 145 attacks on

50   "Church Closures and Arrests Continue in Wa Region, Myannmar." Voice
of the Martyrs. October 22, 2018. https://vom.com.au/church-closures-and-
arrests-continue-in-wa-region-myanmar.

churches which was recorded in the database by the Center for Homicide Research in Minneapolis. At the writing this chapter, our country experienced another horrific attack in Pittsburgh, Pennsylvania, at The Tree of Life synagogue on Saturday, October 27, 2018, when Robert Bowers walked in and killed 11 persons and wounded six. This was a hate crime against Jewish people in their house of worship. Oh yes, the enemy is raging and persecution continues.

Subtle Enemies

The enemies that also plague the average Christian in the Western Christian world is the enemy within. Not that other Christians in other parts of the world do not deal with these foes, but theirs are usually so obviously evil and life threatening. Ours can be more subtle and passive, but are just as dangerous to our faith as the threat of death. These opposing forces enter our senses and take habitation if we do not stay on guard.

I am not talking about being demon-possessed or oppressed. Please note Christians cannot be demon-possessed, but can experience oppression. I am alluding to the fact that there are forces that come against our faith and we must be conscious of them and know how to overcome them. Let us look at three of these adversaries closely so that we can begin to watch and pray over our soul's journey. The theme scripture for this discussion is: 1 John 2:16-17:

> "For all that is in the world, the lust of the flesh, and the lust of the eyes, and the pride of life, is not of the Father, but is of the world. And the world passeth away, and the lust thereof: but he that doeth the will of God abideth forever."

Join me as we unpack these two verses together to understand the plot afoot to undermine the work and the will of God in our lives.

First, these enemies are in the world. What does this mean? Let us look at Verse 15 of the same chapter which says:

> "Love not the world, neither the things that are in the world. If any man love the world, the love of the Father is not in him" (1 John 2:15).

The "world" then, offers a different life than what the Lord wants for us. But it can still be a little foggy when it comes to what is worldly or secular and what is divine and holy. I found this definition which paints the picture clearly.

> "...The world is taken also for a secular life, the present state of existence, and the pleasures and interests which steal away the soul from God. The love of the world does not consist in the use and enjoyment of the comforts God gives us, but in an inordinate attachment to the things of time and sense. We love the world too much (1) when, for the sake of any profit or pleasure, we willfully, knowingly, and deliberately transgress the commands of God; (2) when we take more pains about the present life than the next; (3) when we cannot be contented, patient, or resigned, under low and inconvenient circumstances; (4) when we cannot part with anything we possess to those who want, deserve, and have a right to it; (5) when we envy those who are more fortunate and more favored by the world than we are; (6) when we honor and

esteem and favor persons purely according to their birth, fortunes, and success, measuring our judgment and approbation by their outward appearance and situation in life; (7) when worldly prosperity makes us proud and vain and arrogant; (8) when we omit no opportunity of enjoying the good things of this life; when our great and chief business is to divert ourselves till we contract an indifference for rational and manly occupations, deceiving ourselves, and fancying that we are not in a bad condition because others are worse than we."[51]

To summarize all of this is to say that anything or anyone that pulls my affection, devotion and commitment away from God in worship and service is worldly, carnal or secular. I use the word "carnal" to bring additional clarity to the subject of worldliness. To be carnal means that one is fleshy or lives to please one's appetite and not to please God. It is the opposite of being spiritual, which means to be in obedience to God's Word and God's Spirit. These three enemies purport a worldly, secular or carnal lifestyle. The verse admonishes us not to love the teachings and practices of the world.

The First Enemy: The Lust of the Flesh

Let's start with the **lust of the flesh**, which is mentioned in 1 John 2:16. Lust seems to be the common denominator when speaking about the flesh or the appetites of the human soul. This suggests a drive, a craving, an intense desire to satisfy one's flesh to the point that it pulls that one away

51   McClintock and Strong Encyclopedia, Electronic Database. © 2000 Biblesoft.

from God. This does not only include the obvious sins of adultery, fornication or murder, but it does include the ones that are seemly innocent or harmless.

I remember when I first became a believer at the age of 13. I was living in Harlem, recently migrated from Jamaica, West Indies, and was very lost and lonely in a new country. Settling into this new world was very rough and rocky. I was alone most of the time, because my parents worked, and I spent my evenings doing my homework and waiting for them to come in from work. I became fascinated with all of the soap operas. Programs like "The Secret Storm," "All My Children," "General Hospital" and "Dark Shadows" became my friends. I ran home after school to catch these shows and they became my world, my enjoyment and my fantasy. I lived my life through them. I did not see anything wrong with gravitating towards these persons on the screen and following the storylines, waiting for the outcomes of their decisions and behaviors. I really believed they were harmless or even redemptive, because they were my company and they kept me out of trouble.

When I got saved, however, the Lord challenged me to surrender my addiction to these shows and turn that energy into worshiping Him and studying His Word. Well, I was thoroughly convicted and wept before the Lord. I suddenly saw the hours that I spent pouring my life into something that was not real or beneficial to my soul. There is nothing wrong with watching television, going to the movies or attending a play. What was wrong for me was that it filled a place in my life that consumed me, gratified me and pulled me away from my Lord. He wanted to gratify my soul and become the center of my joy.

I can report victory over this addiction, this lust that had me so spellbound that I would run home religiously and glue myself to the television set. The Lord helped me to replace my love of soap operas with reading, studying the Word of God and becoming very active in my church, which cured my intense loneliness.

Reader, what habit or practice that you are engaged in that keeps you from being close to God and His Word? It could be talking too much on the phone; it could be spending too much time on social media. It could be spending too much time and money in the mall or it could be spending time doing nothing. The Holy Spirit is faithful to bring those things to our attention so that we can repent and change our minds about the matter. Stop and think about what you crave that is out of control!

How Lust Operates

How does lust work in our lives? James 1:14-15 tells us,

> "But every man is tempted, when he is drawn away of his own lust, and enticed. Then when lust hath conceived, it bringeth forth sin: and sin, when it is finished, bringeth forth death."

We can be entrapped with our own desires. They can become so strong and compelling that we become helpless to resist the need to indulge. Look at the simple "sweet tooth" phrase, which describes one's weakness for sweet things. There is nothing apparently wrong with eating sweets, but if you have a medical condition or a dietary issue, eating sweets can obstruct your health goal and be a hindrance to your cause. If having delightful dainties is a must or an obsession, then avoidance or abstinence from this indulgence will not be practiced when lust is in control of the appetite.

Even if the indulgence causes further health issues, when lust is in operation, health concerns will not decide whether one will partake of sugar. Indeed, the drive to satisfy the craving for sweets will be the determining factor.

This habit does not stay contained, as the scripture states, but it becomes more intense, because lust is never satisfied. The more lust gets is the more lust wants. The strong urgings of the flesh should not be ignored. Remember these urgings oppose the work of the Spirit and the Word in our lives. They operate as major distractions and hindrances to the soul of the believer.

> "Now the works of the flesh are manifest, which are these; Adultery, fornication, uncleanness, lasciviousness, Idolatry, witchcraft, hatred, variance, emulations, wrath, strife, seditions, heresies, Envyings, murders, drunkenness, revellings, and such like: of the which I tell you before, as I have also told you in time past, that they which do such things shall not inherit the kingdom of God" (Galatians 5:19-21).

I present this text because the Bible is clear in its identification of fleshly or worldly pursuits. I will not go into it in detail right here, because it would require an in-depth study on each of the aspects of the works of the flesh. The word "works" suggests the workings, the deeds or the way the flesh operates. It describes the way a believer lives when he/she does not follow the Lord. The flesh will automatically function in the lust of the flesh or follow its cravings and desires. The Lord loves us and knows that we are still cloaked in flesh and that we are given to stray from Him every now and then. One of my favorite hymns is "Come Thou Fount of Every Blessing." There is a verse that perfectly describes the propensity of our flesh wandering off from the Lord's leading:

Oh, to grace how great a debtor
daily I'm constrained to be!
Let thy goodness, like a fetter,
bind my wandering heart to thee:
Prone to wander, Lord, I feel it,
prone to leave the God I love;
Here's my heart, O take and seal it;
seal it for thy courts above.

The phrase "prone to wander, Lord I feel it," describes the needs of the flesh, and the restlessness of our inner desires, seeking to be satisfied. The satisfaction that one looks for when the feeling arises will not come from worldly pleasure. If the experience brings pleasure, it will be temporary. Lasting satisfaction in the soul can only come from an ongoing relationship with the Lord. Jesus told the woman at the well in St. John 4 that true satisfaction comes when we worship the Lord in spirit and in truth. He promised the woman that if she received Him into her life, that the emptiness of fleshly pursuits would be quenched by the watering of His presence.

Reader, you may be struggling with a habit, or a sin. You are not hopeless because the power of God is greater than the works of the flesh. Yes, the grace of God working through the Word and the Spirit will sustain you and quiet the flaming of the flesh. As we consider the inflaming and inciting of the flesh, we need to be aware of the things that will trigger and draw out the desires in us and pull us away from the Lord. For some believers it is anger; for others it is money, and for others, it is significance.

Seeking After Significance

Significance seems to be the pursuit of the modern-day believer. Everywhere you turn in the Church, people have a strong, blatantly displayed need to be seen and on stage rather than to serve in obscurity. It has become an epidemic in the church world. Many of the talent discovery shows seem to provoke the urges of hungry souls and stir up the cravings and passions in people to be seen and heard in a great and impactful way. People seek all kinds of creative ways to get recognition and "go viral."

The need for significance can also be wrapped up in the quest to succeed. The world encourages and promotes each of us to strive for the win, secure the gold medal and become the most outstanding. This kind of hype can cause us to have expectations that may not be met, and as a result, will lead us into great disappointment.

In *Search for Significance,* Robert S. McGee writes:

> "We all have compelling, God-given needs for love, acceptance, and purpose, and most of us will go to virtually any lengths to meet those needs. Many of us have become masters at 'playing the game' to be successful and to win the approval of others. Some of us, however, have failed and have experienced the pain of disapproval so often that we have given up and have withdrawn into a shell of hurt, numbness or depression. In both cases, we are living by the deception that our worth is based on our performance and others' opinions — some of us are simply more adept at a playing this game than others."[52]

---

52   McGee, Robert S. *The Search for Significance.* © 2003. Nashville: Thomas Nelson Publishers. Pg. 26.

This kind of drive for approval of significance causes us to look outside of Christ for satisfaction. Author McGee notes why believers forfeit the peace of God and the rest in God by looking to others for approval. One of the reasons for this behavior he calls "Addiction to the Approval of Others" (p. 44). He states:

> "Because other people can give us such approval when we are successful and because we are addicted to obtaining that approval, we often do not want to live only on the approval based on what Christ provided for us. It is not that we should not enjoy the approval of others. The problem is when we have to have it order to live in peace and joy." [53]

This need is a product of the works of the flesh and the motivating factor is lust. Jesus died to dry up these insatiable appetites which push us to ignore the grace that God has given us to live for Him. The scripture states, "...My grace is sufficient for thee: for my strength is made perfect in weakness" (2 Cor. 12:9). The lust, the pull and the propensity to indulge at the expense of our relationship with the Lord will bring nothing but misery. But this scripture tells us that we have the grace and the strength of the Lord to resist the temptations of life.

The Second Enemy: The Lust of the Eyes

The next enemy is noted as the "lust of the eyes." William Shakespeare has been credited with the popular saying, "The eyes are the windows of the soul." In his article, "Your Eyes Really Are the Window to Your Soul," David Ludden, Ph.D., writes:

53   Ibid

"People often call eyes the windows to the soul. But what exactly do we see when we gaze into the eyes of another person? In fact, the eyes do provide lots of information about another person's emotional state. When people are sad or worried, they furrow their brow, which makes the eyes look smaller. Yet when people are cheerful, we correctly call them 'bright eyed.' That's because people raise their eyebrows when they're happy, making the eyes look bigger and brighter."[54]

The eyes in the Bible are the means of getting information. In Matthew 6:22-23, Jesus said:

"The light of the body is the eye: if therefore thine eye be single, thy whole body shall be full of light. But if thine eye be evil, thy whole body shall be full of darkness. If therefore the light that is in thee be darkness, how great is that darkness!"

These two verses tell me that the eye is a receptor of light and information, and it is also a transmitter of that light and that information. The eye can also receive darkness and emit darkness. Therefore, what we see will determine our understanding. It is simply how we see things — through a lens of light or a lens of darkness. Whatever we focus our sight on will determine what focus our lives is on.

But what does the lust of the eyes look like in our daily walk? Reader, we all determine beauty, goodness, love, kindness, strength, power and more through the eyes.

54   Ludden, David, Ph.D. "Your Eyes Really Are the Window to Your Soul," *Psychology Today*, December 31, 2015.

God made this world magnificently and gave us wonderful things to see that reflect His splendor and majesty. The sunrise early in the morning on the landscape of the sky can be the most wonderful sight for our eyes. I am a lover of flowers, and love to visit the Brooklyn and Bronx Botanical Gardens. Walking through those gardens in the springtime is one of my most scenic and breathtaking experiences. The beauty and array of colors speak of God's divine artistry. In the mornings when I rise for my meditation, I sometimes peep out of my bedroom window and catch a view of the birds hopping from limb to limb; I love to see them flying from tree to tree and roaming from bush to bush. Bluejays and robins are my favorites to watch. The colors of their wings lighting up like neon lights in the sun are a marvel to behold.

I travel often and usually sit in the aisle seat, but every now and then I am assigned the window seat. On a clear day, thousands of miles in the air I stare at the clouds and examine their formations. I have allowed my imagination to create figures of animals, humans and nature in the cloud formation. What an amazing God that we serve, who gives us so many wonderful things to behold with our eyes! Even those who are sightless can use their other senses to envision mental pictures of God's earthly landscape.

Yet, this world is also full of evil and my eyes have been unfortunate to behold the display of it. I have seen pain, sorrow, anger, hurt and even death. Yes, the eyes can experience good and evil. As believers, however, our eyes must be guarded to seek God's good. We want pretty things and many things; but often too many things cause us to be more into things than into God. He did not give us all these things to behold so that we would forget Him.

The Western world is obsessed with what we call beauty. Beauty to most people has to do with shape, color of skin, height and perfect bone structure. It is what magazines sell us and we buy it. We conclude something is beautiful and good by what the media says, by what Hollywood does and by what the fashion designers present. We have allowed our eye gates to receive any and everything without running it through the radar of the Word of God.

We are a society of consumers. The greed and craving that we have for things and more things have skyrocketed in our society. Carolyn Gregoire, in her article, "The Psychology of Materialism, And Why It's Making You Unhappy," states:

> "More money, more problems? It might just be true. Americans today, compared to 55 years ago, own twice as many cars and eat out twice as much per person, but we don't seem to be any happier because of it. Rather than rising levels of well-being, we've seen mounting credit card debt and increasing numbers of self-storage facilities to house the things we compulsively buy.
>
> "The holidays in particular have become a time when consumer culture comes out in full force. Black Friday, the annual post-Thanksgiving discount shopping spree, results each year in multiple deaths and injuries of consumers trampled by crowds in stores and shopping malls."[55]

This is definitely a product of the lust of the eyes. Yet, this is not the only example of what our eyes are glued to, which

---

55   Gregoire, Carolyn. https://www.huffpost.com/entry/psychology-materialism_n_4425982. Published 12/15/2013. Updated December 6, 2017.

unglues us from the sight of God. As mentioned in a previous chapter, this social media culture has such a pull on our eye gates that our eyes are constantly fastened to an iPhone, iPod or computer. As gadgets become more high tech, the seduction becomes more intense. Hours are spent on Facebook, Instagram and on other media hosts sharing any and everything about personal, trivial and sometime important information. The social media has become an obsessive way of communicating, giving and receiving information. For some, it is the only way they relate to others. This trend of social media craving has captivated our eyes.

Whenever I take the children out to dinner, I announce that there will be no texting, phone calls or video game during dinner time. If that statement isn't made, everyone's head would be face down with eyes fastened on their phones or gadgets.

The *Forbes* magazine report, "Six Ways Social Media Affects Our Mental Health," by Alice G. Walton, addresses health, medicine, psychology and neuroscience. She wrote:

> "...The American Academy of Pediatrics has warned about the potential for negative effects of social media in young kids and teens, including cyber-bullying and 'Facebook depression.' But the same risks may be true for adults, across generations. Here's a quick run-down of the studies that have shown that social media isn't very good for mental well-being, and in some ways, it can be pretty damaging."[56]

---

56   https://www.forbes.com/sites/alicegwalton/2017/06/30/a-run-down-of-social-medias-effects-on-our-mental-health/#4db8799f2e5a . June 30, 2017.

The report mentions several ways social media is unhealthy for our society: it's addictive; it triggers more sadness; it encourages less well-being. Also, as mentioned previously, comparing our lives with others is mentally unhealthy, and can lead to jealousy and a vicious cycle. We get caught in deluded thinking, and finally, more friends on social doesn't mean we're more social.

These thoughts are worth considering, because we tend to spend more time staring into these gadgets than in the Word of God. Of course, social media has a positive and progressive place in our world, but unfortunately a good thing can be used in the wrong way. Reader, what are your eyes fastened on? What is it that you see that you must have to the point that your affections are moved away from the Lover of your soul, Jesus Christ?

The famed adage, "Children live what they see," is not just an old wives fable; it actually happens. Reader, there are things that you are thinking, feeling and doing as an adult that you gathered from what you saw in childhood. Some of these things are good. Many times, however, they were damaging to our emotions and lives. The unfortunate thing is that sometimes we pass on the ugly and painful sights we have received to the next generation.

The Creative Power of the Eyes

Please study Genesis 30:25-43. In this narrative of Jacob and Laban, we find Jacob, after several years of hard labor, planning to move on with his family away from his father-in-law's home. He makes an agreement with Laban concerning his salary that Laban has never honestly given him. Jacob, therefore, devised a way to separate from Laban with some means to take care of his growing family, which would be in the form of a flock comprised of sheep, lambs and goats.

What would determine which portion of the flock would go to Laban and which portion would go to Jacob? Because Laban was very tricky, Jacob decided to determine a fair share for both. He stated that the members of the flock that had striped marks and spots would go with Jacob and the solid-colored flock would go to Laban and his sons.

Although Laban pretended to agree with this plan, he instead seized all the flock that matched this description and sent them on a three-day journey with his sons. How, then, would Jacob get the young, healthy fertile flock that remained to become striped and spotted? Genesis 30:37-39 gives us the answer:

> "Jacob, however, took fresh-cut branches from poplar, almond and plane trees and made white stripes on them by peeling the bark and exposing the white inner wood of the branches. Then he placed the peeled branches in all the watering troughs, so that they would be directly in front of the flocks when they came to drink. When the flocks were in heat and came to drink, they mated in front of the branches. And they bore young that were streaked or speckled or spotted" (NIV).

So we see that Jacob peeled the poplar, hazel and chestnut tree branches and carved designs in the bark so that they had white stripes and colored spots. He then placed them in the water troughs. The flock, while in a mating moment, was brought to the water to drink. While they were mating, conceiving and drinking, they were looking in the water at these white speckled and striped barks. These items caught their eyes, registered in their minds and became part of their reproductive system. Consequently, they produced a flock that was striped and speckled.

It is a powerful testimony of how our eyes take pictures of life and register and repeat it in our spirits. It also shows that at vulnerable times in our lives, it is easy to reproduce what we have seen and conceived. The essence of this story exhorts us to be aware of how powerful our eyes are and the way we process thoughts and live out deeds. Therefore, we must guard our eyes from looking at, yearning after and reaching for anything that would cause us not to reproduce Christlike living. Keep your eyes on Christ and into His Word.

How many car accidents have been caused because people did not keep their eyes on the road and looked somewhere else? The newest enemy to car accidents is not drunk driving but phone texting. It is an epidemic that the motor vehicle registry calls "distracted driving." Looking at the phone while driving can be just as fatal to someone's life as being intoxicated while driving. What has distracted you when you were supposed to keep your eyes on Christ? When have you experienced an "accident" as a result?

Let me now share a portion of my favorite hymn, which hopefully will encourage you to focus your eyes in the right direction. Helen Howarth Lemmel shared this gem entitled "Turn Your Eyes Upon Jesus." Here is the refrain of that hymn:

> *Turn your eyes upon Jesus,*
> *Look full in His wonderful face,*
> *And the things of earth*
> *will grow strangely dim,*
> *In the light of His glory and grace.*

"Look full in His wonderful face" means to focus on Who Jesus is and how you can live to please Him. Just place your hand over your eyes right now and ask the Lord to shift them from the attraction of the world and place them on the beauty and wonder of our Lord and His presence.

The Third Enemy: The Pride of Life

The third enemy of your godliness is the pride of life. What does this text from 1 John 2:16 mean when it says, "the pride of life?" The word "pride" in the Greek language is *alazoneia*, which Vine's dictionary says is "arrogant display, or boastings." James 4:15-16 says:

> "For that ye ought to say, If the Lord will, we shall live, and do this, or that. But now ye rejoice in your boastings: all such rejoicing is evil."

This scripture clearly states that when we depend on ourselves and leave God out of our plans, we have crossed over into pride and empty self-confidence. This dictionary really unpacks the meaning and expression of pride by saying:

> "Pride is inordinate and unreasonable self-esteem, attended with insolence and rude treatment of others... Pride manifests itself by praising ourselves, adoring our persons, attempting to appear before others in a superior light to what we are; contempt and slander of others; envy at the excellences others possess; anxiety to gain applause; distress and rage when slighted; impatience of contradiction, and opposition to God himself."[57]

---

57 McClintock and Strong Encyclopedia, Electronic Database. © 2000, Biblesoft.

Pride, therefore, is self-centered, self-seeking and self-confident. We are all victims of pride. When Adam and Eve disobeyed God, the whole human race fell into that disobedience. Everyone that is born has the desire, propensity and will to be locked into self rather than to surrender to God. Pride, therefore, is not just isolated acts of selfishness, but it is embedded in our nature to think more of ourselves than to think of God. This self-preservation is taught to us from birth. We are raised to protect, provide and promote self.

Is it so wrong to care for oneself? Is it wrong to promote one's dream or passion? Is it ungodly to seek the best for oneself? The answer to all of this is that nothing is wrong with any of it within moderation. Pride and arrogance have to do with excessive amounts of attention and elevation of self. Pride is all about self and considers little or nothing about anyone else. The mother of pride is selfishness. If you do not believe this, look at how selfish we become when we feel as if we are losing or not having our way. Listen to the language we use and the thoughts that we have when our person is threatened. We immediately go into self-protective or self-preservation mode. We are born with this response; it is intrinsically embedded in our nature.

This is readily seen when children are playing together. One child pulls a toy from the other and the other child attempts to take the toy back. This tug-a-war continues until someone has the toy and the other one does not have it. The resulting language may be non-verbal, which often becomes screams, sobbing and what we call "temper tantrums." In this setting, the child's self is threatened, therefore, his/her ego is assaulted.

Children often engage in this narcissistic behavior which

is their attempt to deal with their reality. It is generally accepted by adults, thinking that they will grow out of it as they learn that they are not the only one in the world. Unfortunately, many people remain stuck right there, because they are still self-seeking and self-wanting. This is just a part of our human nature, but when we are born again, the Holy Spirit goes after this need and challenges us to live differently from the way we naturally function. This new way opposes pride and presents to the Christian heart the spirit of humility. Humility confronts pride; it pulls it down and keeps pride in check.

Reader, I could use so many other individuals' testimonies on pride, but I am not sure they would want me to write about it. Therefore, in this book I refer to my own experiences because the memory of them is so vivid in my mind. I recall the early days of my church experience at the Greater St. John Pentecostal Church in Harlem, under the leadership of the late Bishop Lenora Smith. I was enamored with church and found so many friends in that community. I was considered the "deep one." I was always at the altar praying; always reading my Bible; always involved in the Bible studies and always asking questions about the Word. I was so saved in my mind, that I did not know that I was self-righteous.

One of the young men said to me one day that he wanted to marry me. I turned around in disdain and shouted: "I would not marry you if you were the last man on earth." It was not what I said but how I said it. You see, he did not have a job and I turned my nose up at him because I believed that being jobless was not what I would want to be attached to or desired. As I said before, it was not what I said, but how I said it. Most young women want to be married to a man who is gainfully employed. No one wants to get into a relationship without any apparent security. But, it was the superiority that rose up in the breast; it was the scorn that was expressed in the tone of my voice, and it was the arrogance with which I phrased my words. Yes, pride can be expressed and lived out in a nasty way.

Well, without question, the Lord heard me. He was determined to deal with this attitude in me. He just waited for the right time and the right situation. I ended up marrying a man outside of the Faith, who, by the way, never held a job for any considerable length of time. While I was in that terribly dysfunctional marriage, I remembered my nasty attitude towards that young man. It is not about whether I accepted his expression of intent, but my self-righteous, proud, "holier-than-thou" attitude that I demonstrated in that moment. During my unhealthy marriage, I was confronted with this spirit of pride, and by the time the marriage was over, I was very conscious of how awful self-centeredness could be. I am sure you also have your stories of how pride puffed you up and caused you to hurt others or hurt yourself.

While I was writing this chapter, a friend sent me an article about pride. (How timely!) Fabienne Harford, a contributor to desiringgod.org, wrote an article entitled "Seven Subtle Symptoms of Pride." She states:

> "Pride will kill you. Forever. Pride is the sin most likely to keep you from crying out for a Savior. Those who think they are well will not look for a doctor. As seriously dangerous as pride is, it's equally hard to spot. When it comes to diagnosing our hearts, those of us who have the disease of pride have a challeng-

ing time identifying our sickness. Pride infects our eyesight, cause us to view ourselves through a lens that colors and distorts reality. Pride will paint even our ugliness in sin as beautiful and commendable. We can't conclude that we don't struggle with pride because we don't see pride in our hearts. The comfortable moments when I pat myself on the back for how well I am doing are the moments that should alarm me the most. I need to reach for the glasses of Christlike humility, remembering that nothing good dwells in my flesh, and search my heart for secret pride and its symptoms."[58]

Harford quoted the theologian Jonathan Edwards, who wrote one of his essays pointing out seven sneaky symptoms of the infection of pride. I chose one of the symptoms to look at with you, which is *desperation for attention*. The article states,

"Pride is hungry for attention, respect, and worship in all forms. Maybe it looks like being the person up front boasting. Maybe it looks like being the person who is unable to say 'no' to anyone because you are hungry to be needed. Maybe it looks like thirsting for marriage, or a better marriage, because you are hungry to be made much of."[59]

Jonathan Edwards continues,

"People often tend to act in a special manner as though others ought to take great notice and regard

---

58 http://www.fabsharford.com/7-sneaky-symptoms-of-pride.
59 Ibid.

of them. ...It becomes natural for him to expect such treatment and to take much notice if a person fails to do so, and to have an ill opinion of those who do not give him that which he feels he deserves."[60]

The notion of self-seeking worship is a very strong component of pride. What is the definition of worship?

"Honor, reverence, homage, in thought, feeling, or act, paid to men, angels, or other 'spiritual' beings, and figuratively to other entities, ideas, powers or qualities, but specifically and supremely to Deity."[61]

This act of worship should be given to God and God alone. The Lord gave the children of Israel the Ten Commandments. The first demand has to do with how He wants them to worship Him and Him alone, which Exodus 20:4-6 states:

"Thou shalt not make unto thee any graven image, or any likeness of any thing that is in heaven above, or that is in the earth beneath, or that is in the water under the earth: Thou shalt not bow down thyself to them, nor serve them: for I the Lord thy God am a jealous God, visiting the iniquity of the fathers upon the children unto the third and fourth generation of them that hate me; And shewing mercy unto thousands of them that love me, and keep my commandments."

---

60   Edwards, Jonathan. "Undetected Spiritual Pride: One Cause of Failure in Times of Great Revival." http://www.grace-abounding.com/Articles/Sin/Pride_Edwards.htm.

61   "Worship." Bromiley, Geoffrey W., Ed. *International Standard Bible Dictionary.* 1988. Grand Rapids, MI: Eerdmans.

This command clearly defines who should be worshipped and what the worship should look like. This worship should be exclusively given to the Lord. Humanly, however, when we feel needy and desperate for unrealistic attention, an overwhelming need for self-protection, and a driving force for personal entitlement, we may reach out for excessive devotion. We all need to feel secure, accepted and recognized. But when those needs are not centered in the will of God and covered by the Word of God, then we will seek out ways to become the center of attention.

Yet like Hagar, striving for mastery and at odds with her mistress Sarai, we will only find peace and true fulfillment when we bask in the attention of the One Who sees and knows us intimately, and turn our eyes completely upon Him:

> "And she called the name of the Lord that spake unto her, Thou God seest me: for she said, Have I also here looked after him that seeth me?" (Genesis 16:13).

Affirmation and attention means too much to the saints these days. The Body of Christ and the world is loaded with the necessity for affirmation. It is so strong that it's almost disgusting. Everyone must be affirmed, recognized and have their territory. But there really is no territory, Saints. It all belongs to God. No one is winning but Him. He won at Calvary! So ultimately, no one should receive the attention, accolades and applause but Him. When you live like that, your spirit is free, and you don't have a whole lot of gas, digestive issues, and spiritual ulcers.

Reader, you may have been in the midst of people who do all the talking and the talking is only about them, ignoring other people's presence and importance. They are so overtaken by themselves that they are unaware of people's disinterest. The excessive drive for being the only one with the only need can ruin a relationship. Many marriages can be affected negatively because of this. Many talented athletes, musicians and skilled workers cannot get along with people or succeed in their field because they cannot work in a group setting. The center of it all is pride. This feeling of wanting so much more in so many ways will bring disappointment and frustration to the seeker. Only God can quiet the urges and the surges of self-praise and self-exaltation.

The Problem of Pride

Please be reminded that the spirit of pride comes from the devil. It was pride that caused him to be kicked out of heaven. This passage describes the adversary's pride and arrogance in Isaiah 14:12-14:

> "How art thou fallen from heaven, O Lucifer, son of the morning! how art thou cut down to the ground, which didst weaken the nations! For thou hast said in thine heart, I will ascend into heaven, I will exalt my throne above the stars of God: I will sit also upon the mount of the congregation, in the sides of the north: I will ascend above the heights of the clouds; I will be like the most High."

The language is very pictorial and pungent, as it describes the enemy's drive for exaltation and promotion in the face of Almighty God. It is also seen in Matthew 4:8-10:

> "Again, the devil taketh him up into an exceeding high mountain, and sheweth him all the kingdoms of the

world, and the glory of them; And saith unto him, All these things will I give thee, if thou wilt fall down and worship me. Then saith Jesus unto him, Get thee hence, Satan: for it is written, Thou shalt worship the Lord thy God, and him only shalt thou serve."

These two passages openly show that the devil wanted what belonged to God. This insatiable need was passed on from the devil to Adam and Eve and then to us. It is laced through our being, and if we are not born again and walking in godliness, it will scream out for uncontrollable gratification, which leads to destruction. In your spare time, please read the following passages, which talk about the danger of a prideful life: Proverbs 11:2, 13:10, and 16:18.

I will conclude with this scripture which always brings me to my knees, and I hope will challenge you in the same way. It is the latter clause of 1 Peter 5:5:

> *"...for God resisteth the proud, and giveth grace to the humble."*

There are two kinds of people presented in this text; the proud and the humble. The proud is haughty and tries to outdo others. God will always resist, put Himself against or oppose them. The humble, however, meaning the person who walks in submission to God, or is lowly, God will always extend favor or graciousness.

Reader, don't you want the approval of God; the favor of His presence and the assurance of His pleasure? If so, you will have to surrender the lust of your flesh, the lust of your eyes and the pride of your life to the superintending of the Holy Spirit and the Word of God. In doing so, you will be assured of God's continuing peace, joy and righteousness. This assurance is what brings a great sense of contentment and rest in your heart and mind. Stop right now and pray this prayer with me:

> *Dear Father,*
> *In the Name of Your Son Jesus Christ, I come to You honestly and openly hiding nothing but surrendering everything. Please search my heart, mind and soul and reveal to me the hidden places where the enemies of my faith lurk and hide. Show me myself, heal me and teach me in a new and fresh way! When You do these things, I will ever praise, worship, and adore You. I will talk of Your wondrous work of deliverance in my life and help those who need to experience You in their life. Amen! Amen!*

CHAPTER NINE

A Contented Life: Rest for My Soul

Hush, my heart and calm your fears
Jesus is here, so very near
Life with its billows dashes and roars
Leaves me so battered, weak and sore
But there is quietness beyond compare
There is a stillness penetrating the air
It is the peace that God affords
To all who will trust Him more and more!
- J. McCULLOUGH

TRAVELING FROM place to place, city to city, country to country and church to church can take its toll upon me physically, emotionally and spiritually. I have slept in many different hotels, but there is no place like sleeping in my bed. When I get home from a trip, I seek to find rest, peace and quiet. This rest is so important to me, because it is in the rest that I am refreshed, renewed and restored. The demands of life, the business of work, the management of home and family, and the activities of church and ministry can rob us of having body rest and soul rest. Even Jesus had to go and steal away and find solace while He was engaged in Kingdom service and encouraged His disciples to go with Him (Mark 6:31). The word "rest" here means "restore, refresh and repose." This is necessary for everyone to experience in this life of hustle, bustle and stress. This chapter, however, is more about rest for the soul. I am not minimizing the necessity to take care of the body, to nourish the body or relax the body. But the body can appear to be relaxed, while the soul is in turmoil.

It's easy to be in turmoil when we are hating our lives and experiencing so much personal dissatisfaction. Some of our personal conditions, situations and life circumstances cause us so much dread, dismay and loathing that we become resigned and hopeless. Others often brood and sulk, becoming angry, vengeful and bitter. It is almost as if we are serving time, and completing a prison sentence. We desperately desire to escape, and wonder when or even if we will encounter release or breakthrough.

The Psalmist David cried out in Psalm 42, expressing the agony of his pain, fears and disappointments. He even described his intense thirst and desire for God to fill the emptiness of his soul. David's inner being wrestled, strove and roared deeply against him. This inner turmoil caused him much misery and discomfort. After a while, he concluded that only praising God in it would bring healing and calm to his existence. I am sure that we can identify with David, while considering our own troublesome times and challenging moments. I call this place of rest **"contentment."**

A Contented Place of Grace

One of the texts in the Bible that encourages this contentment is 1 Timothy 6:6, "But godliness with contentment is great gain."

We have discussed the subject of godliness and ungodliness in previous chapters. Now, we will talk about the companion to godliness, which is **contentment**. What is contentment? The *Strong's Concordance* notes the entry NT:841 for the Greek word *autarkeia* (ow-tar'-ki-ah) as "a competence or sufficiency." I like *Unger's Bible Dictionary's* treatment of contentment which states:

> "The word means 'sufficiency' and is so rendered in 2 Cor. 9:8. It is that disposition of mind in which one is, through grace, independent of outward circumstances (Phil. 4:11; 1 Tim. 6:6,8), so as not to be moved by envy (James 3:16), anxiety (Matt. 6:24,34), and discontent (1 Cor. 10:10)." [62]

This definition points to a key component of contentment or satisfaction — and that is grace. This contentment cannot be achieved through ordinary or natural means. It is only through the grace of God issued to us through the death of His Son Jesus on the Cross that we find rest for our souls.

A new job with more money cannot do it; a new relationship with someone special will not do it; a new location with a fresh start has no power to do it. The only way the believer finds rest and peace, or a hush for their innermost being is by accepting the grace that has been offered to us by Jesus Christ.

What is grace? Grace is the undeserved favor that was given to every believer when Jesus died on the Cross. It is when God decides to show us kindness when we least deserve it. We deserved eternal separation from God, but

---

62 "Contentment." Biblesoft's New Exhaustive Strong's Numbers and Concordance with Expanded Greek-Hebrew Dictionary. © 1994, Biblesoft and International Bible Translators, Inc.

God's mercy offered up Jesus on the Cross and Jesus' Blood washed away our sins and rendered us not guilty in the sight of God. This is what this marvelous grace, favor and abounding love has done for us eternally.

Grace though, is not only for salvation, but it continues to operate in our lives to bring us more and more into the life of Christ. His favor is available to us to enable us to live freely and fully in the peace and love of God's care. Paul declares in Colossians 2:9-10:

> "For in him dwelleth all the fulness of the Godhead bodily. And ye are complete in him, which is the head of all principality and power."

This literally means that Jesus is fully God and has everything that we need in Him. We, therefore, who are believers, have everything we need because Jesus lives in us. This "everything" makes us complete. This word "complete" in the Greek means "to satisfy, furnish and to make full."

With this in mind, we should ask ourselves why we are not contented. Why are believers so restless, angry, miserable and confused? Why are we still searching for life's answers from secular sources? Why are we rejecting biblical guidance and counsel and reaching for worldly sayings and meanings? Why are we so angry at God and the way He operates in our lives? These are the questions we must ask ourselves earnestly, because these are the issues that have compromised our walk with the Lord. Let's look at the word "sufficiency" in 2 Corinthians 9:8:

> "And God is able to make all grace abound toward you; that ye, always having all sufficiency in all things, may abound to every good work."

There's that word "grace" again. God is all-powerful, which means He is able, and is not lacking the ability to give you what you need when you need it. The word "abound" denotes that the supply of grace or favor will not come as little drops but will come in abundance.

Now, when we talk about abundance in the Church today, we usually mean prosperity or financial blessings. But this sense of grace also addresses the power to live free from depression, chronic frustration and continual hopelessness. Reader, if you do not believe that the grace of God is able to keep your heart and mind in the midst of difficulty, you will not have peace, calm and contentment. You will simply live in pursuit of the material and reduce your Christian walk to something joyless, mundane and laborious. I challenge you to partake of our Father's abundance for your soul — mind, will and emotions.

The will of God for our lives is that we should have sufficiency in all things. "Sufficiency" is the same word for "contentment," meaning in every situation I can be at rest. Reader, you may ask, *How does one find rest in the midst of unrest?* You may also say that I have no clue about the hardship you have endured in the past or are experiencing right now.

Many believers have strayed away from the Faith because they are not convinced that peace can be experienced while enduring severe conflict. When adversity arises, believers often are ill-equipped to stand. Many of the teachings of the Church have caused believers to stop believing and caused unbelievers to avoid believing. We have been exposed to what people are calling "fake church," and now we are defecting or trying to defect from the Faith by abandoning God, the Church and the Word of God. Defecting from the Faith is not the answer for the believer. The way to find rest in a world of evil, hate and destruction is to be contented with God in our souls.

Contentment is Not Settling

To some, contentment is a dirty word, because it is some-times equates with settling. One of my ministers, Rev. Su-zette Parchment, shared on exhortation with our church on the thought that if there is one thing we absolutely cannot stand and do not like, it is the thought, idea or feeling that we are settling. It is a source of outrage and anger to know that we could have done, been, or received better. We hate to think that there is something more that is owed to us, and even worse, that someone has the nerve to withhold it from us. "We often don't mind if someone else is settling our debt in our favor, but we hate if we feel we're settling," says Rev. Suzette. But being content and settling are not synonymous.

In settling, you may be owed more, but you agree to ac-cept or receive less. Or you may owe more, and the other party agrees to receive or accept less from you. Rev. Su-zette discussed settling in the context of debt collection, and also in the context of relationships. "You may owe your husband or wife more, but you don't give it, and they accept less," she shared.

But here's what contentment is — what I have, I am satisfied *with* it, and I am satisfied *by* it. I don't need any-thing further to hit the spot. Rev. Suzette states, "I could go further and get more, but I don't feel the need to because what I already have is sufficient for me. I accept what I have, who I have, and where I've been placed with joy. " With con-tentment, I don't always feel the need to reach for the next upgrade to make me happy. She said, "I don't live my life on a leash always looking for the next best thing. I can be satisfied with the 2015 version of the latest gadget even though it's 2019, because it continues to meet my need."

In other words, ladies and gentlemen, we don't live our lives on the prowl. Some of us live our lives on the prowl for the next best thing. We do it because there is something within us that is not satisfied, happy or content, and if we don't get what we want, it means we have settled. Many times we have difficulty in giving, not only money, but even of ourselves, because there is something faulty about our godliness and appropriate belief about God.

It seems as if today's charismatic church stresses grace to get things, but not to flesh out the power of Christ in our daily lives. For example, let us look at forgiveness, which is a popular topic for Bible teaching, counseling and relationship discussions. Yet it can be the most misunderstood concept within the Church community. Some say that they forgive but won't forget; others say they will only forgive if the other person changes, and many others say that forgiveness is too hard and painful. This is where God's promised abounding grace manifests itself to all who will believe. Let's examine this truth in the life of Corrie Ten Boom.

Grace to Help

Corrie Ten Boom and her family lived in Holland during World War II during the rise of Nazism. She and her family were arrested for hiding Dutch Jews in their home from the Nazis. They all went to a concentration camp in Germany at Ravensbrück, and were treated inhumanely as women and were forced to walk naked in front of the Nazi soldiers. They were also mocked and whipped with leather straps.

Years later, when the war was over, Corrie survived and

started speaking publicly on forgiveness. After her presentation, a gentleman approached her and identified himself as one of the guards in the camp that brutally abused the victims. He extended his hand and said he was now a believer and asked her to forgive him. She had just finished teaching on the subject and was faced with the challenge to practice what she taught. She asked for the help or the grace of God to help her, which allowed her to shake his hand and receive a tremendous healing and deliverance from a horrible past.

This is all written in her book, *The Hiding Place*, which I highly suggest that you read in your spare time. Is Corrie Ten Boom a superwoman? Is she especially anointed to forgive? No! She just believed that the grace of God would give her the ability to do what humanly and naturally she could not do.

This is what brings peace and rest to troubled souls. This is grace in action and available to help in the time of need. May you stop right now and look within your heart and see what area you need to surrender to the grace and love of Christ so that your soul can find rest and peace. Corrie did not have time to ponder or get a therapy session; she only whispered a prayer to the God Who gives us what we need freely and abundantly. It is not always money, but it is guidance, strength and divine help. If your heart is open to receive from the Lord, you also can experience grace to help for whatever you may face.

Getting back to the definition that we mentioned before from *Unger's Bible Dictionary*, we learned that our contentment cannot be dependent on outward circumstances. This is not just a churchy statement, but a biblical fact. Just think logically for a minute! If we have everything we need, the way we want it, when we want and how we want it, then there wouldn't be any need for prayer, faith or help from the Lord. We would be self-sufficient. How then would we get to know Him, trust Him and believe Him? It is through the adversities and sufferings that we get to see Jesus as our Helper and Deliverer. We try to hold onto things and people, but there is no guarantee that things and people will last. There is little or no sufficiency in what we have and what we strive to have.

My mother lived to be 105 years old. She was bedridden and unable to attend church. Yet all the way up to her nineties, she was fussy and particular about her clothes, shoes and wigs. She had her Sunday clothes laid out on Saturday nights and everything had to match and be in pristine condition. She also had her jewelry organized and displayed for her to make her selections. But, when she came to the end of her days, and prepared to transition to the other side, she did not ask for any of her treasured or favorite possessions. She started worshiping and turning her gaze towards heaven. She was not interested in any earthly ownership but looked towards her eternity.

> "For we brought nothing into this world, and it is certain we can carry nothing out" (1 Tim. 6:7).

Please don't get uptight when I talk about holding on to things or possessions! I know we need earthly things to live here while we are alive. This scriptural admonition is not suggesting that we should neglect ourselves and ignore our needs for clothes, shoes, food, shelter, transportation, education and recreation. God promised to take care of our needs and provide for our lives.

The issue, however, is when we depend on the accumulation of these things to make us happy or fulfilled. This dependency can become an obsession to the point that we live to have more and more. True contentment is choosing to be happy with what we have, knowing that we are not defined by our possessions.

Jesus admonished His disciples about properly valuing possessions by saying:

> "And he said unto them, Take heed, and beware of covetousness: for a man's life consisteth not in the abundance of the things which he possesseth" (Luke 12:15).

Evict Envy

You are not what you have, but Whose you are! To experience contentment, one has to avoid or keep envy at bay. Envy is an enemy to our peace, rest and joy. It can create a tremendous amount of unrest and a drive to compete. The Greek New Testament word for "envy" is *phthonos*, which denotes a strong feeling of discontentment due to selfishness and creates a drive to want what someone else has. This is due also to covetousness, which we talked about in a previous chapter, but is worth mentioning again.

This plague that I call envy can destroy relationships, ministries and homes. This soul malady is caused by a deep sense of discontentment and dissatisfaction, with a little pinch of greed. When believers refuse to trust God, rest in His Word and believe His promises, they may become preoccupied with other people's lives, possessions and relationships. This preoccupation with "others" can become an obsession and cause an unbelieving soul to behave out of control. This out-of-control behavior can express itself in so many unhealthy ways. James describes what this behavior leads to in James 3:16: "For where envying and strife is, there is confusion and every evil work."

Envy is different from jealousy. Jealousy means that we want back what someone took from us, but envy wants to possess something that belongs to someone else. Envy incites strife, meaning it creates contention. One English dictionary describes contention as "heated disagreement." Envy causes one to be at odds with people, out of sync with arrangements and argumentative and disgruntled.

Please remember that the believer's life is planned and orchestrated by the Lord. He is the one and only Sovereign and is seated as Lord and Ruler over the whole earth. He knows just what we need and where to take us. When we do not believe this, we will feel neglected, abandoned and rejected. We begin to resent our life; we end up hating our journey and seeking another kind of life.

Meet Miss S. She is a young 23 year old, recently graduated from college. She is bright, attractive, progressive and ambitious. She believes that she is entitled to a certain job in her field with a certain salary and benefits. Yet it has been two years and she has had to settle for a job away from her expertise for far less pay than she expected. She has many prophecies that her blessing is great beyond measure and that it was right at her door. She is now very depressed, angry and very disappointed.

She has a brother, also a recent graduate, who has landed a six-figure job within two weeks of submitting his application. She loves her brother, but lately she has become contentious. She has stopped praying, reading her Bible, and going to church. She feels cheated and forgotten. All the promises that she once believed have now become a cause for frustration.

Miss S. was never taught that God is in charge, and delay does not mean His denial. She was never told that every believer will be tried and tested to see if they can trust God when things are not what they expect. Disappointed, she not only withdrew from her brother, but also criticized and competed with him. She is manifesting contentious behavior due to envy; her desire to receive what her brother had and believed she deserved to have mastered her and she hates her life.

The only way Miss S. can get her joy, hope and peace back is by agreeing with God about her circumstances and accepting His blessing and His guidance. The whole notion of contentment is based on trust. I cannot say this enough. When I trust the Lord, my heart will rest in His choice for me and believe that this choice is made for me because He loves and cares for me.

> "Trust in the Lord with all thine heart; and lean not unto thine own understanding. In all thy ways acknowledge him, and he shall direct thy paths. Be not wise in thine own eyes: fear the Lord, and depart from evil. It shall be health to thy navel, and marrow to thy bones" (Proverbs 3:5-8).

Putting the Axe to Anxiety

To become content, we must ask God to help us master the urge to become anxious. In Philippians 4:6, we are warned not to be anxious about anything. This anxiety is called "distracting care." In other words, we should not become so overly concerned to the point that it robs us of our peace and rest. We are to be concerned about our responsibilities and exercise stewardship over all that God has given us. The key point here is that God grants earthly stewardship to us and we must trust Him to tell us how to manage what we have. If we trust ourselves, when it doesn't work, we may become discouraged and dismayed. But when our hearts are seeking those things that are above, we remain calm and in the peace of God.

Anxiety, which is excessive worry or preoccupation with a situation, cannot change our circumstances, nor bring peace and quietness to our souls. It only heightens fear and doubt. It creates problems, but never brings solutions; it makes assumptions without facts and it encourages possibilities before actualities. When I am anxious, I imagine the worst before I have any reason or proof of the outcome.

I cannot fret and trust at the same time. Fretting requires much emotional, physical and psychological energy. It can rob me of sleep, and affect my eating patterns. It can change the status of my vital signs and it can set the stage for mental pressure. An article from Harvard Health Publishing on "Anxiety and Physical Illness" states:

> "Understanding and treating anxiety can often improve the outcome of chronic disease, such as GI tract problems and heart disease... Anxiety has been implicated in several chronic physical illnesses, including heart disease, chronic respiratory disorders, and gastrointestinal conditions. When people with these disorders have untreated anxiety, the disease itself is more difficult to treat, their physical symptoms often become worse, and in some cases they die sooner."[63]

---

63 https://www.health.harvard.edu/staying-healthy/anxiety_and_physical_illness. July, 2008 and updated May 9, 2018.

The feeling of anxiety, if it continues, can be very dangerous to body, soul and spirit. How then can we maintain our joy of spirit, contentment of soul and peace of mind? Philippians 4:6-7 tells us how to exercise these preventative measures:

> "Be careful for nothing; but in every thing by prayer and supplication with thanksgiving let your requests be made known unto God. And the peace of God, which passeth all understanding, shall keep your hearts and minds through Christ Jesus." (Philippians 4:6-7).

The Antidote for Anxiety

The first step is to pray to God about the matter. The word "prayer" is translated "to worship, prostrate or fall down before the Lord and talk to Him about the problem."

The next step is to supplicate, which means to petition or plead. This kind of prayer is a persistent asking without ceasing. It is praying relentlessly and seeking an answer without wavering.

This, then, is followed with thanksgiving or speaking well of God, telling Him how good, kind and faithful He is. This thanksgiving is the key, because before we receive the blessing, we must be assured that God will give us what is best for us and be willing to articulate it.

This is how we shift our energies from anxiety to faith, from doubt to trust and from despair to hope. The petition that we make with faith in Almighty God will bring about physical, emotional and spiritual benefits which will undergird our contentment and joy.

The result of this spiritual activity will bring about desired result. In Philippians 4:7, it declares that the peace of God, meaning His grace, His life and His comfort will bring us a quietness of the soul that cannot be experienced without His presence. This calm repose will guard us from excessive alarm; overactive responses and compulsive decision making. It will cause us to "be still and know that [He] is God" (Psalm 46:10). Scripture tells us this peace will act as soldiers guarding our heart and mind even when we are asleep.

This is contentment is beyond compare. It defies the realities of our circumstances and creates a safety net for our minds and emotions that is almost inexplicable. God is so awesome that even in the worst of times, when we go to Him for help, His help can supernaturally manifest itself at the time of our need.

A friend of mine went to the doctor for her regular physical exam. A few days later, she received a call from the doctor, who gave her a very grave diagnosis. She was overwhelmed with fear, apprehension and stress. She called and I prayed with her. The Lord led me to assure her that she should wait and get another test to be sure if this is really what the problem is. The spirit of anxiety was trying to rob her by creating more images of despair in her mind.

Before the day was out, she received a call from the doctor saying it was another patient's information that was given to her and that it was not her diagnosis. She received the peace of God and the blessing of the Lord, because she went to Him in prayer.

We are not alone. We do not have to carry these heavy burdens, because He is a Burden-bearer. Written as a poem in 1855 to comfort his mother who was living in Ireland while he was in Canada, this traditional hymn by minister Joseph M. Scriven always comforts my heart, especially this first verse:

What a Friend we have in Jesus,
all our sins and griefs to bear!
What a privilege to carry
everything to God in prayer!
O what peace we often forfeit,
O what needless pain we bear,
All because we do not carry
everything to God in prayer!

Joy, peace and contentment are the benefits that we will receive from the Lord as we draw closer to Him. These benefits are immeasurable and priceless. We cannot pay for this spiritual privilege with money or performance. We have to trust and obey so that we can be happy in Jesus.

Given the information on how to embrace contentment, we should now seek to shake off all the shackles of envy and anxiety and reach for the security and safety of the Word of God. Change the very atmosphere of your home by saturating it with praise and worship! Attend your church service consistently; read your Word and apply it daily! Serve the Lord and the community faithfully! If we continue in this path of trusting, believing and obeying, then we will not become so dissatisfied with our lives and behave as if God has been cruel and mean towards us. Count your blessings and recall your deliverances. Look back and be grateful! God has never forsaken or forgotten you. Every step of the way, He has been faithful. Jeremiah states that every morning that we wake up, new and fresh mercies we receive. His faithfulness is great, and His love is steadfast. Hold on to this and resist the temptation of discontentment, fear and unrest.

CHAPTER TEN

The Benefits of Contentment

NOT THAT I SPEAK IN RESPECT OF WANT:
FOR I HAVE LEARNED, IN WHATSOEVER STATE I AM,
THEREWITH TO BE CONTENT.
PHILIPPIANS 4:11

CONTENTMENT DOES not come naturally to the human heart! Why? Because, we are compassed about with so many situations in life and experience so many changes along the way that it is hard to maintain a state of contentment and satisfaction of spirit and soul. This contentment or state of fulfillment can only be experienced through intentionally maintaining an intimate ongoing relationship with the Lord Jesus Christ. In the previous chapters, we talked about all the issues surrounding contentment, but now we will talk about the levels of satisfaction and how it benefits the soul.

Paul made a very powerful statement in Philippians 4:11-13. He was very blessed to receive care packages from the church at Philippi while he was in prison. There were times though, when this church did not have the means to give to him consistently. They gave when they had it. He was very grateful and thanked them from his heart. Prisoners are usually very dependent on the care of their outside family and friends. They often expect to receive gifts which reflect love and consideration from their community. When these gifts or care packages stop coming in, it is very easy for the prisoner to become discouraged and to feel abandoned.

I have a brother who is incarcerated, and we are very careful to let him know that he is not forgotten or forsaken. We often send him personal things that he needs so that he will feel cared for, thought of and cherished. Yes, sharing is caring. Paul, however, knew how to live with a certain attitude of joy and peace whether he received anything from the Church at Philippi or not.

Contentment in Abasement

How did this incarcerated preacher maintain his contentment and satisfaction? Please note that this was the only church that thought about him as he suffered many beatings, experienced much rejection and endured many reproaches for the preaching of the Gospel. People, cities and homes were changed spiritually because of Paul's preaching and teaching. Yet, this is the only church that really cared for him in the hour of his need.

Paul should have felt abandoned, discouraged, angry or even bitter. But instead, he was calm and at rest in his soul. Many of us would be outraged that we gave to so many people and they forgot us in the time of distress. There are people that you and I know who are very sad and distraught because they were neglected or forsaken. These feelings can run so deep that if ignored, they cause much emotional pain and spiritual barrenness.

Paul talked about a certain kind of benefit that the grace of God afforded him so that he could navigate through the different moments of life without deep regrets or grief. To understand this divine impartation of strength of mind and rest of soul, we need to look closely at the text.

The first clause of Philippians 4:11 states: "Not that I speak in respect of want." This means that when he thanked the church for their help, he also acknowledged that he was not upset with them when he did not receive from them. He was not responding to them out of want. He was not desperate or suffering from destitution. How could that be for a man in prison, who needs all the help that he can get? What he was saying was that he was not begging or so needy to the point that he became depressed or angry. His necessity did not control his life.

The question still stands as to how did he go through this with a godly attitude? Philippians 4:11b says, "...for I have learned, in whatsoever state I am, therewith to be content." This state of mind came through instruction from the Lord. The instruction clearly states that whatever state he was found in, he had learned how to be content, meaning satisfied and at peace. The word "learned" means that sometime in the past, he became informed and understood how to be content where he was and with what he had. Only the Spirit of the Lord with the Word of the Lord can teach that kind of lesson.

The learning points to Paul's attitude and decision to trust in God's providential care. Paul recounts to the Corinthians some of his trials of ministry:

> "In journeyings often, in perils of waters, in perils of robbers, in perils by mine own countrymen, in perils by the heathen, in perils in the city, in perils in the wilderness, in perils in the sea, in perils among false brethren; In weariness and painfulness, in watchings

often, in hunger and thirst, in fastings often, in cold and nakedness" (2 Cor. 11:26-27).

Paul learned and understood how to endure difficulties and hardships, which enabled him to find peace while enduring a storm. *Barnes' Notes* declares in its commentary:

> "A contented mind is an invaluable blessing, and is one of the fruits of religion in the soul. It arises from the belief that God is right in all his ways. Why should we be impatient, restless, discontented?" [64]

Paul found his sufficiency in the Lord and therefore was not dependent on his circumstances. You may be going through trials right now and everything around you is out of control. The enemy, people and your mind are telling you that your life is not worth anything. Remember, you have learned from past experiences with the Lord that He has never left you alone. You have learned patience and strength even in the midst of it all. Well, I celebrate the fact that you are experiencing divine help and support from the Holy Spirit.

Paul further helps us to understand the benefits of being contented and having our sufficiency in the Lord by declaring in Philippians 4:12:

> "I know both how to be abased, and I know how to abound: everywhere and in all things I am instructed both to be full and to be hungry, both to abound and to suffer need."

The instruction that Paul received is the same instruction that is available to us today. God desires to show us how

64   "Philippians." Barnes' Notes, Electronic Database. © 1997, Biblesoft.

to really live without being trapped in our challenging situations and live a life of hopelessness. The word "abased" means he had learned how to live humbly. This means he had found the secret of life, the patience in trouble and the peace in turmoil. These are the benefits or profits of contentment and rest in the Lord.

Paul, as we mentioned before, went through many humiliating situations, but the lessons learned made him rise above and did not allow it to define him. He was able to put earthly things in their proper place because of a heavenly perspective and viewpoint:

> "If ye then be risen with Christ, seek those things which are above, where Christ sitteth on the right hand of God. Set your affection on things above, not on things on the earth. For ye are dead, and your life is hid with Christ in God" (Colossians 3:1-3).

What is it that you may be going through that seemingly is trying to define you, confine you and deter you? Whatever it is, please listen for the voice of the Lord. You can emerge out of it with new strength and a clear mind when your affections are set above.

Most believers know the story of David and how he was a shepherd boy anointed by Samuel as a teenager to be king over Israel. However, he did not get to the throne until about 17 years later, because Saul was still on throne for many years. During the time of his waiting to get to the throne, he and his 600 men lived as fugitives. Roaming the hills of Judea, he protected the farmers and landowners from bandits.

Let us revisit again the account in 1 Samuel 25. David

asked a landowner by the name of Nabal for some provi-
sions for him and his hungry men. Nabal blatantly refused
and verbally humiliated David. Needless to say, David became enraged and plotted to kill Nabal and those in his
household. David was anointed, but hungry, disillusioned
and disappointed. This experience could have caused David to become bitter, vengeful and murderous. The natural
thing for David to do at this time would be to take revenge,
and this was his desire. He was humiliated and repulsed by
the refusal of Nabal. Indeed, he was tempted to cut off all
the males of the house, and verbalized his intent to do so:

> "So and more also do God unto the enemies of David,
> if I leave of all that pertain to him by the morning light
> any that pisseth against the wall" (1 Samuel 25:22).

Yet David was now set up to learn how to be satisfied
with how God was leading him. How? He was counseled by
the wife of Nabal, Abigail, who encouraged him not to allow
insults, resistance and rejection to define him. She reminded him that God promised to take him to the throne. So even
if he was humiliated then, he would be exalted later.

Well, years later, David became king over all Israel. But
he had to learn how to endure abasement and still head towards his life's assignment. In this, he was instructed to be
patient, to be contented and to be hopeful. That moment
when he could have given up and forfeited his purpose
through anger and revenge, he heeded the advice from Abigail and went on to fulfill his purpose. Every humiliation
leads to transformation and completion.

Contentment in Abundance
The other portion of the text also stated that Paul ex-

perienced contentment when he abounded. What does "abound" mean? It means that Paul also learned how to handle God's blessing, but more so blessings in abundance. This indicates an over-and-beyond supply and provision from the Lord.

What is the lesson that Paul learned in prosperity? He learned not to let the blessing become an idol. He learned that having much should not crowd out the need for God or the presence of the Lord. He learned that all good gifts come from the Lord; therefore he was always aware of the goodness of the Lord and gave his life freely and sacrificially to the Lord. Paul's rest was not in riches or abundant blessings. He understood that in life blessings come and blessings go, but the Lord remains faithful.

This is the secret of contentment and satisfaction of the soul. A contented soul has information that the average person does not have. In the passage of Scripture that we examined, Paul repeatedly said he "knew" how to be contented under any circumstances. The secret, then, is *knowledge*.

What is the knowledge that kept Paul's heart and mind steadfast on the Lord? The Word of the Lord states in Isaiah 26:3, "Thou wilt keep him in perfect peace, whose mind is stayed on thee: because he trusteth in thee." The benefits are peace, sufficiency, completeness and hope. This cannot be found in things, people or achievements, but only in trusting the Lord.

To trust in the Lord is to lean, depend and rely on the character of God through His Word and Spirit. This confidence in God reflects the believer's knowledge of God's ability to perform, transform and fulfill His will and walk fully as His disciple. When we rest in this knowledge, we find rest for our souls. I encourage you to lean fully on Him in every area of your life, that you may be able to walk in the fullness of contentment.

I Hate My Life

So yes, as we consider the words of our Savior, we are indeed called to hate our lives.

> "And there went great multitudes with him: and he turned, and said unto them, If any man come to me, and **hate not** his father, and mother, and wife, and children, and brethren, and sisters, **yea, and his own life also**, he cannot be my disciple. And whosoever doth not bear his cross, and come after me, cannot be my disciple" (Luke 14:25-27).

The multitudes were drawn by the fishes, loaves and miracles of healing, but Christ challenged their hearts and made a greater and higher demand. He does the same with our hearts today. The Greek word translated "hate" means "to love less." Consider whether you prefer Him above all. Is the Lord alone your chiefest joy? Our joy must rest in Him alone Who is greater, wider, larger than anything we could ever dream or imagine. Our affections must be set on Him Who is above, so that we might fulfill His divine calling in the earth that He might draw all men to Himself.

The Peace Benefit

We don't have to look far to experience turmoil, tragedy and conflict. There are times when I choose not to view the news because it brings such unrest to my mind and spirit. Peace is a godly commodity that is attainable even in these troubling times. The contented heart can find unusual peace and "rest," even in the midst of conflict and upheaval. How is this possible? The report concerning increasing rise in mental health problems has caused even the Church to become concerned about the well-being of people's minds.

On October 4, 2001, the World Health Organization (WHO) reported from Geneva, "One in four people in the world will be affected by mental or neurological disorders at some point in their lives. Around 450 million people currently suffer from such conditions, placing mental disorders among the leading causes of ill-health and disability worldwide."[65]

This alarming report causes everyone to look at the deficits that we are experiencing in our lives emotionally and spiritually. The believer may also experience stress, depression, anxiety and confusion. These emotions rob the born again Christian of his/her peace. The text in Isaiah gives us the answer as how to experience personal peace in a world of chaos.

> "Thou wilt keep him in perfect peace, whose mind is stayed on thee: because he trusteth in thee" (Isaiah 26:3).

The One Who gives this peace, which has nothing to do with our external circumstances, is God. God will preserve, protect and sustain His people with perfect peace. The word "peace" is *shalom*, which means "safety, health, rest and prosperity." The text also says "perfect peace." What does "perfect" mean here? It just means "peace, peace."

This double dose of peace is what we need in these times

---

65   The World Health Report : 2001 : Mental Health : New Understanding, New Hope. https://apps.who.int/iris/handle/10665/42390.

of innumerable chaotic situations that occur daily. Only the contented, trusting believer full of faith in God can experience this kind of peace in varied moments. The only way to practice this peace is to do what the text says. God will keep us in "peace, peace" if our mind is stayed on Him. That is the secret and benefit of a contented heart and mind.

How do I keep my mind stayed on him? The word "stayed" in the Hebrew is OT:5564 - *camak* (saw-mak'); to prop (literally or figuratively); reflexively, to lean upon or take hold of (in a favorable or unfavorable sense): KJV - bear up, establish, (up-) hold, lay, lean, lie hard, put, restself, setself, stand fast, stay (self), sustain[66]. This definition is quite clear on how to gain peace.

But the text gives a key word on how to lean, or rest on the Lord. The word is "trust." This word is to put confidence in and reliance on the Lord. This is the essence of contentment. Trust God's Word and follow the leading of His Spirit, which guarantees peace under any circumstances. This peace will not come by osmosis; you can only know it because of the way you think about God and the way you respond to His guidance. This is one of the greatest benefits that you and I can have because we are contented with Him and we are not resisting His purpose for our lives.

Consider the thoughts of Pastor John Piper as he talks to us now about peace from a very familiar passage of scripture — John 14:27:

> "'Peace I leave with you; my peace I give to you. Not as the world gives do I give to you. Let not your hearts be troubled, neither let them be afraid.' So in the last

---

66   Strong, James. Strong's Exhaustive Concordance of the Bible. Abingdon Press, 1890. Print.

hour of his life, Jesus is helping you not be anxious.

"'Let not your hearts be troubled.' The peace He has in mind might include global, national, political, intra-ethnic or inter-ethnic peace. Those aren't at the front of his mind, though, and I know it isn't because of what he says: "Peace I leave with you; my peace I give to you. Not as the world gives do I give to you. Let not your hearts be troubled. He goes on to say: 'The peace that Jesus gives is not circumstantially based. It is peace in bad circumstances.'

"'Not as the world gives.' How does the world give peace? It does. The world gives peace with retirement accounts. The world gives peace with health insurance. The world gives peace with bomb shelters. The world gives peace with safety nets in the society. The world gives peace with police. The world gives peace of mind in a hundred ways, which I'm thankful for and I'm glad they exist. And Jesus says, 'I'm not giving that way. That's not what I'm doing.' 'What do you mean, Jesus, that you're not doing it that way?' The peace that Jesus gives is not circumstantially based. It is peace in bad circumstances, in tribulation, in no health insurance, and in police breakdown — in societal breakdown. It's in these things we have peace — the peace that passes all human comprehension.

"Why did Paul call it that in Philippians 4:7? What does that mean? That means human beings can't grasp it, and they can't make it happen. God makes it happen."[67]

---

67   Piper, John. "Perfect Peace for Anxious Souls" | Desiring God, https:// www.desiringgod.org/messages/my-peace-i.../perfect-peace-for-anxious-souls. July 25, 2018.

Pastor Piper has shared with us the way we can keep our peace and walk in this benefit of contentment.

The Hope Benefit

The Center of Suicide Prevention reports that suicide is the fourth leading cause of death among children between the ages of 10 and 14. How can this be among our children? I am not even mentioning adults, teenagers and believers. Suicide seems to have become a very attractive option even for professing Christians. I will not mention here the number of preachers who have taken their lives while actively involved in ministry.

I sincerely believe that hopelessness plays a great part in the consideration of or involvement in suicide. I pray that this chapter helps someone to overcome hopelessness. I am noting this in this chapter because contentment of the heart, soul and mind helps one to overcome hopelessness.

Let us look at hope, which will help us to appreciate contentment differently. In the New Testament, hope is defined as the "expectation of good" (Grk. *elpis*).

> This original word denotes a joyful and contented expectation of eternal salvation (Acts 23:6; 26:7; Rom. 5:4-8; 1 Cor. 13:13). Because of God's manifested salvation in Christ, and because He is the source of all the believer's expectations, He is called the "God of hope" (Rom 15:13)."[68]

I love the expression "joyful and contented expectation." You see, being contented or at peace with God's plan and

---

68   *The New Unger's Bible Dictionary.* Originally published by Moody Press of Chicago, Illinois. © 1988.

purpose drives away the notion that we are hopeless, neglected, forsaken or abandoned.

The example that comes to mind is found in Psalm 42:11,

> "Why art thou cast down, O my soul? and why art thou
> disquieted within me? hope thou in God: for I shall
> yet praise him, who is the health of my countenance,
> and my God."

David was being pursued by his enemy and felt hopeless
and helpless. But because David had a relationship with
the Lord, he did not remain in that condition, but he did
what we should do when our contentment is threatened.
He asked himself the question, *Why?* He dealt with the
signs of hopelessness, which is a cast-down soul and a disquieted spirit.

What is a cast-down soul? It means a depressed soul
which is sinking down on the inside. David's soul was de-
pressing itself. This depression can be caused by negative
talk; hopeless thoughts; overwhelming fears and nagging
anxieties. His spirit was disquieted within him, meaning
there was a war, rage or a commotion ravishing his inner
being. These feelings were self-inflicted.

But, because David was a worshipper, he climbed out of
the abyss of his emotional darkness by declaring that he
would hope in the Lord, which means that he would patiently wait and trust in Lord.

He also knew that the way back to contentment was to
praise the Lord. The word praise is *yadah,* which means to
extend one's hands to God, expecting to receive, confess-
ing one's faith and receiving one's help. David walked away
from this experience stating that this is how he keeps a

healthy disposition or a life of wholesomeness and wellness.

Reader, this is another benefit of having a spirit of contentment; where nothing can easily rock your world or cause you to be chronically bent out of shape. Again, I look to the hymns to speak from my heart when it says:

> *On Christ the solid Rock I stand*
> *All other ground is sinking sand*
> *All other ground is sinking sand*

I pray that your life will be influenced to draw closer to the Lord and be at peace with Him as you read through this book. In this life we are pulled, tossed and shaken by adversities, challenges, defeats, but also victories. Whatever, and wherever betide us, we can be found knowing that the Lord is on our side and will bring a peace that passeth all understanding when we yield our lives to Him. This assurance is based on His steadfast love, which is not based on our goodness or performance. It is strictly and freely founded upon His desire to have us as His own. Respond fully to His wondrous love and grace today.

This is a wonderful opportunity to confirm and reaffirm your commitment to Him, as you receive His love and tender favor. Continue to hold on to this truth as you cherish His presence and rely on His care. Share it with someone else who may be hurting. You never know who you will be able to aid as you allow the Lord in His love and care to overshadow you in His counsel and comfort.

Philippians 4:13 declares Paul's affirmative statement and confession of Faith. He declared that he could do all things through Christ Who gives him abounding strength. Whether in humiliation and defeat, or success and victory,

Paul could endure without being shaken or moved by these states. Why? Because of the strength of Lord in his life, Paul could move from one end of life's spectrum to the other, and still stand firm in his belief. You can be assured that with the Holy Spirit living inside of you, fueled by the Word of God, you will be enabled to find rest, trust and stillness of soul in any and every situation. This is not just Paul's testimony; it can be yours from this day on.

Let us conclude in prayer:

> *Father, in the Name of Your Son Jesus,*
>
> *Help us to find rest in midst of a world of evil and despair. We know that You have called us to love You, live for You and serve You. It is Your will that we live a life of satisfaction and rest in You. We often get sidetracked, but Lord we are coming back to the comfort of Your arms and the assurance of Your love. Help us to let nothing separate us from Your truth, Word and presence. When we walk closely with You in prayer and devotion, our heart receives rest and stillness from every difficult place. Thank You, Lord, for the contentment that will keep us from a hopeless life!*
>
> *In Jesus' mighty Name we pray, Amen!!!*

Made in the USA
Middletown, DE
02 September 2019